The Civil War for Kids

The Civil War

★ ★ ★ FOR ★ ★ ★

Kids

A HISTORY WITH 21 ACTIVITIES

★

JANIS HERBERT

CHICAGO
REVIEW
PRESS

Library of Congress Cataloging-in-Publication Data

Herbert, Janis, 1956—
The Civil War for kids: a history with 21 activities / Janis Herbert.
    p.   cm.
    Includes bibliographical references (p. 142) and index.
    Summary: Teaches about the Civil War from the secession
debates to Appomattox, by means of activities like making butternut dye, decoding wigwag, and baking hardtack. Includes a
resource section with a glossary and pertinent web sites.
ISBN 1-55652-355-6
1. United States—History—Civil War, 1861–1865 Juvenile literature. 2. United States—History—Civil War, 1861–1865—Study
and teaching—Activity programs Juvenile literature. [1. United
States—History—Civil War, 1861–1865. 2. Handicraft.] I. Title
E468.H55 1999
973.7—dc21   99-20826
                                                        CIP

© 1999 by Janis Herbert
All rights reserved
First edition
Published by Chicago Review Press, Incorporated
814 North Franklin Street
Chicago, Illinois 60610

ISBN 1-55652-355-6

Designed by Joan Sommers Design, Chicago
Printed in Singapore by CS Graphics
5 4 3 2

To the boys, Arnie and Paul, who always let their little sister play too.

Contents

Acknowledgments

Thanks to Sara Dickinson, Lois Germond, Mark Homstad, Signe Murphy, Rodney Powell, and Jason Williams who graciously offered encouragement, information, and resources for this book. I'm grateful to David Martinson for his cheerful support and his Southern perspective, and to Linda Ivey Miller for sharing her ancestors and her knowledge of American history. Thanks to James Burgess, Chris Calkins, Rick W. Hatcher III, Donald C. Pfanz, and Terry Winschall of the National Park Service, and to Robin Reed, Museum of the Confederacy, who provided helpful information for this work. Ted Alexander and D. Scott Hartwig kindly offered recommendations that made this book a much better one; I'm very grateful for their knowledge and gracious assistance. Many thanks to Donna Younger, who improved my work and whose love for history and literature has been an inspiration. Mark Stephens so generously gave of his time and knowledge that a new category of thanks seems in order. His help was invaluable; he has my heartfelt gratitude. Thanks to designer Joan Sommers and to all those at Chicago Review Press who worked hard to make this book a reality. Special thanks to Cynthia Sherry and Rita Baladad for their enthusiasm and devotion to this project. I'm grateful to Ruth and Don Ross for their constant encouragement, assistance, and support. To my dear husband Jeff, who never tires of hearing about the Civil War, thank you for helping me to follow my heart.

Timeline

1619	Slaves sold in Virginia
1808	Importation of slaves outlawed
1820	Missouri Compromise
1852	Publication of *Uncle Tom's Cabin*
1854	Kansas-Nebraska Act
1857	Dred Scott Decision
1859	John Brown raids Harpers Ferry
1860	Abraham Lincoln elected President
1861	FEBRUARY Confederate States of America formed
	APRIL 12 Attack on Fort Sumter
	JULY 21 Battle of Manassas (Bull Run)
1862	FEBRUARY 6 Fort Henry falls
	FEBRUARY 16 Fort Donelson surrenders
	MARCH 9 Battle of the *Monitor* and the *Virginia*
	APRIL 6–7 Battle of Shiloh
	APRIL 25 New Orleans falls
	MAY 31–JUNE 1 Battle of Seven Pines (Fair Oaks)
	JUNE 26–JULY 2 The Seven Days' Battles

BROADSIDE FOR SLAVE AUCTION, 1829

JOHN BROWN

THE CAPITOL UNDER CONSTRUCTION, 1860

GUN SQUAD ON THE DECK OF THE *MONITOR*

THE BATTLE OF SEVEN PINES, 1862

LINCOLN ON THE BATTLEFIELD OF ANTIETAM, 1862

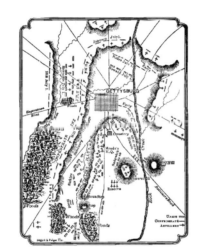

MAP OF THE BATTLE OF GETTYSBURG

THE RUINS OF ATLANTA, 1864

GENERAL LEE LEAVING APPOMATTOX

Note to Readers

See the Glossary following Chapter 14 for an explanation of unfamiliar terms. In the resource section you will find a list of officers of the Confederacy and the Union for quick reference.

Introduction

Not long ago, a great war was waged in our nation, the United States. Your great-great-grandfather might have been a soldier in this war. Your great-great-grandmother might have plowed fields while her husband fought, or served as a nurse on the battlefields. This war was fought on their land, in their small communities. Their farms became battlefields and their homes were turned into hospitals. Towns were divided, and sometimes families were too. Brothers fought against brothers, fathers and sons were on opposing sides, and schoolmates and old friends faced each other in battle.

This war, the Civil War, lasted four years. Three million Americans fought in over 10,000 battles and skirmishes across the country. More than 620,000 soldiers died. Those who fought suffered greatly in this war that seemed to have no end.

What was it that led a once-united people to wage such a long and terrible war? The practice of slavery divided the nation and caused people to struggle over the basic principles upon which the country had been founded. They went to war to decide whether we would continue to be a nation and, if so, what kind of nation we would be.

The deeds of the soldiers and the people of this time are told, briefly, here. You'll learn about the terrible battles the armies fought—Antietam, Chancellorsville, Gettysburg. You'll find out what it was like to hear the drum rolls, see the flags unfurl, and "Forward march!" into battle. Along the way, you'll learn how to send signals and decode messages, make a soldier's lean-to shelter, drill like a private, and command like a general.

So join Clara Barton as she tends the wounded at Antietam . . . Joshua Lawrence Chamberlain as he shouts "Fix bayonets!" to his brave men at Gettysburg . . . nine-year-old drummer boy Johnny Clem as his drum is smashed at Shiloh . . . Generals Robert E. Lee and Ulysses S. Grant as they lead their men in the great Civil War. Because of these heroes, the United States was reborn with a new understanding of freedom and union. Join them in the greatest struggle our country has known.

1

To War!

The Union Is Dissolved

In 1861, citizens gathered in town squares all across the country to hear speeches about freedom, states' rights, and glorious death on the battlefield. In the North, bands played rousing versions of "Rally 'Round the Flag," and young men jumped at the chance to fight for union. In the South, "The Bonny Blue Flag" inspired men to defend their rights and their land. The country was divided in two.

The split had been a long time in coming. Many events led to the great Civil War of the United States, but the main reason so many fought and died was the practice of slavery. Slavery—the South's answer to its need for a large, cheap labor force to raise its main crop, cotton—was a source of terrible friction between North and South. Many slaves led lives of back-breaking labor, poor rations, and beatings. Their lives were not their own. They were property,

like a horse or a wagon. They could be sold at any time and separated from their spouses and children.

The North and South were like two separate countries. The growing North attracted immigrants to its bustling cities and manufacturing jobs. The South was an agricultural land, and its proud and aristocratic people wanted nothing more than for it to remain that way. Not all Southerners were slave owners, but the South's

Harriet Tubman

Slaves escaped on the "Underground Railroad"—not an actual railroad, but a network of routes to the North, with safe stops along the way. Harriet Tubman escaped slavery but risked her freedom to help others. In 19 trips, she led more than 300 people out of bondage. Slave owners offered thousands of dollars for her capture.

Tubman was so good at disguising herself that when she saw her old master again, even he didn't recognize her.

This "conductor" on the Underground Railroad was called Moses, after the Biblical prophet who led his people out of captivity. During the war Tubman was a nurse and a scout for the Union.

economy depended on the large cotton plantations worked by slaves. Without slavery, Southerners feared their whole way of life would be destroyed. The friction between the regions grew.

A group of people began calling for the abolishment of slavery. They became known as "abolitionists." As this abolitionist anti-slavery movement grew, the federal government outlawed importation of slaves and tried to limit slavery to the South. Southerners felt their country was turning against them and threatened to "secede" (withdraw) from the United States and form their own country. To calm them, Congress passed a Fugitive Slave Law in 1850. Under this law, escaped slaves who were captured in the North could be claimed as property and taken back to captivity. People could be jailed for helping slaves escape. Abolitionists were outraged. Harriet Beecher Stowe was so upset that she wrote a novel about the plight of slaves. Her story became the most popular book of its time. *Uncle Tom's Cabin* was such a powerful book that Abraham Lincoln would call Stowe "the little woman who wrote the book that made this great war."

An American Slave Market,
1852

Frederick Douglass

Douglass was born a slave. His mistress started to teach him to read, but stopped when his master said it would make him an unfit slave. Determined to learn, Douglass gave his food to boys on the streets in exchange for help spelling out words.

Disguised as a sailor, he escaped on a ship to the North, where he lectured, wrote an autobiography, and started an abolitionist newspaper. Douglass encouraged Lincoln to free the slaves and recruited black soldiers for the Union army.

Whenever I hear anyone arguing for slavery, I feel a strong impulse to see it tried on him personally.

—ABRAHAM LINCOLN

In the new western territories, the debate about slavery turned violent when a new law allowed the settlers to decide whether to become a slave state or a free state. More than 200 people were killed as slavery and anti-slavery forces battled over the fate of the territory soon to be known as "Bleeding Kansas." Blows even fell in the Senate, where a Southern congressman beat an abolitionist senator with his cane! The issue of slavery was in newspapers, in public debates, and on everyone's mind. Then, in 1857, a case argued before the Supreme Court divided the country even more.

Missouri slave Dred Scott often traveled with his master, and for a time they lived in the North. Scott sued for his freedom on the basis of having lived in free territory. His case reached the Supreme Court, which decided that blacks were not citizens and therefore had no right to sue. It ruled that Scott and other slaves were private property, and that their owners could take them anywhere. Scott was freed by his owner two months later, but slaves throughout the South would have to wait another eight years for their freedom.

Two years later John Brown pushed the country closer to war. This abolitionist tried to begin a slave uprising in Harpers Ferry, Virginia.

With a small group of men, including his sons, he took over the federal arsenal and captured a large store of weapons. During the struggle several men were killed, including Brown's sons. A lieutenant colonel in the U.S. army named Robert E. Lee arrested Brown, who was found guilty of treason by the state of Virginia and hanged. Brown's actions were illegal but his motives were noble, and they inspired admiration among many Northerners. Though he was found guilty, Southerners were mortally offended by the North's praise for his actions.

As the election of 1860 came near, it was clear that the issue that would decide the outcome was slavery. Four candidates ran for the presidency in that year. A remarkable man from Illinois, Abraham Lincoln, won the election.

Lincoln was born in a Kentucky log cabin. His mother died when he was a child, and his family barely scraped a living together. He attended school for only one year but, between chores, he read every book he could find. As a young man, he tried many trades—flatboat man, clerk, postmaster, soldier, surveyor—before becoming a lawyer. Many people in the country were surprised when this country lawyer won the presidency. Some thought he was too rough and undignified (Lincoln loved to tell jokes and

> **A house divided against itself cannot stand.**
> **I believe this government cannot endure**
> **permanently, half slave and half free.**
> **It will become all one thing, or all the other.**
>
> —ABRAHAM LINCOLN

Lincoln's Beard

Before becoming president, Lincoln was clean-shaven. What inspired the change? During the campaign he received a letter from 11-year-old Grace Bedell, who said he would look a great deal better if he let his whiskers grow. Lincoln wrote a reply to Grace, and when he went through her town on the way to Washington he stopped to show her his new beard.

Abraham Lincoln

funny stories), but he was a man of great intelligence and wisdom. With his wife, Mary Todd, and their three boys, Lincoln left Illinois on a train bound for Washington. He was about to lead the United States through its most difficult time.

Lincoln's train trip to Washington was eventful. His son Robert happily rode with the engineers. They stopped in towns across the country and crowds gathered to see the man who would lead the nation. He visited Grace Bedell in New York and gave a stirring speech at Independence Hall in Philadelphia. Someone saw him playing an undignified game of leapfrog with his sons Willie and Tad at a Buffalo hotel. Everywhere, there were parades in his honor. In one town, a cannon salute shattered the windows of Mary Lincoln's train car.

Death threats haunted them on the journey. Lincoln was warned to stay away from Baltimore, Maryland, a city with sympathies for the Southern cause. The presidential train was sent through the city without Lincoln aboard. Dressed in a large overcoat and a soft hat, Lincoln slipped into a carriage, then entered Washington on another train.

Choosing Sides

The Civil War was fought between 23 Union states and the 11 states of the new Confederacy. In 1861, Virginia and West Virginia were one state. When Virginia seceded, the western part of the state broke away to side with the North and became West Virginia.

The 33 states that were in the Union in 1860 had dwindled to 27 by Lincoln's inauguration in March 1861. The Southerners wanted no part of a Union that would elect an anti-slavery president, and they felt they had the right to break away from the United States. Not so long before, Americans had written a Declaration of Independence, claiming their freedom from British rule and the right to choose their own government. In the Constitution, they outlined the principles of the new government, including protecting its citizens' right to life, liberty, and the ownership of property. Southerners felt that attempts to free the slaves were unconstitutional and that the government was taking away their rights. Since people should be free to choose their own government, Southerners felt that secession was within their rights. They said it was no different from the actions of George Washington and the Founding Fathers.

Northerners didn't agree. The states had joined together in union and agreed to abide by majority rule. Now the Southerners were leaving because they didn't get their way. Northerners wanted to be sure that this government by the people and for the people continued to exist. If the South was allowed to secede, the United States would be a failure.

The month before Lincoln's inauguration, the Southern states formed their own government, the "Confederate States of America," and inaugurated a president, Jefferson Davis. At the time Mississippi seceded, Davis was its senator.

Jefferson Davis

Like Lincoln, he had been born in a Kentucky log cabin. His family later moved to a plantation in Mississippi. Jefferson Finis Davis was the last child in a family of 10 and his parents gave him a middle name announcing the fact (*finis* means "the end" in Latin)! He attended the U.S. Military Academy at West Point, served in the

Union Yankees and Confederate Rebels

Northern troops were called Union soldiers, Federals, or Yankees. The Southern men who fought for the new Confederate States of America were the Confederates. They were also called Rebels, because they had rebelled against the Union.

Map of United States in 1861, showing the division of North and South

Mexican War, was a congressman, a senator, and secretary of war for the United States. The tall, thin Davis predicted at his inauguration that the Confederacy and the United States it had just parted from would go to war, a "war long and bloody." Southerners felt that Davis, with his iron will and fierce loyalty to the Southern cause, was the perfect man to lead their new nation.

Lincoln hoped to avoid war but knew that preserving the Union might require it. Northerners were confident that if it came to war, their victory was certain. In 1860, 30 million people lived in the United States. Twenty-one million were Northerners. The Confederacy held only nine million and, of those, four million were slaves. The South was rural, "the land of cotton," and had little industry. The more industrial North could manufacture the supplies it needed for war. It had more railroads, and was in control of the seas. The South had advantages, too. To conquer the South, Northern armies would have to invade a large land with long coastlines. Many

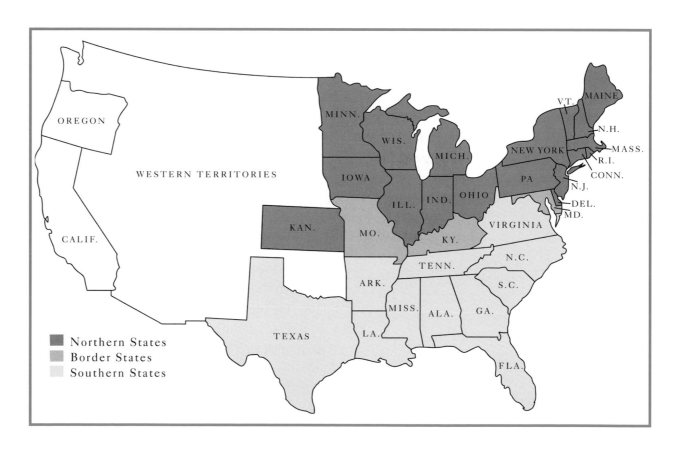

Southerners were from farms and knew how to handle guns and horses, unlike urban Northerners. More had been in the military and military schools. Most important, the Southerners would be fighting to protect their homes, making them the fiercer opponents. Southerners felt they could whip the Yankees and be back home in no time.

Attack on Fort Sumter —April 12, 1861

When Confederate forces fired on the federal post of Fort Sumter in Charleston, South Carolina, war became a reality. The Confederate government wanted the federal troops to abandon the fort, which was in what they considered to be their country. After 34 hours of relentless shelling, Major Robert Anderson of Fort Sumter surrendered to Southern General Pierre Gustave Toutant Beauregard—one of his former students at West Point.

The surrender of Fort Sumter electrified the people of the North and the South. Lincoln called for 75,000 men to serve for 90 days. Men volunteered in droves. War! They wouldn't have missed it for the world. War fever swept the nation. How dare the Southerners secede! Why, it was no less than anarchy! When Lincoln called

for volunteers, more Southern states left the Union. Virginia seceded and Richmond became the capital of the Confederacy. Jefferson Davis moved his children and his wife, Varina, to the new Confederate capital. So many men volunteered to join the Southern army that some were turned away. States' rights and liberty were at stake! The sacred right to self-government was what this country was founded on. They'd fight and die for that right. To war!

Union and Confederate troops clashed in various places over the next few months. In Missouri, Confederate sympathizers fought furiously against Union troops. Skirmishes in towns across Virginia quickly brought the reality of war home to the citizens there. The first major battle of the Civil War, however, was Manassas, or Bull Run.

There were so many volunteer soldiers in Washington that there was nowhere to put them. Some even set up camp in the chambers of the House of Representatives! They arrived just in time, for the Confederate camps of the Southern soldiers were just across the Potomac River. The capitals of the two nations were uncomfortably close, less than 100 miles apart.

The Union troops were untrained and would need time before they could be ready to fight. The Northern people, though, were ready for bat-

Spies Everywhere

Spies disguised themselves as peddlers, clergymen, or other everyday characters. Women and children smuggled messages in their hair, or in hollowed-out wedding rings and dolls. Fugitive slaves spied, too. In Washington, Rose Greenhow charmed military secrets from an admirer and relayed them to the Confederates. Actress Pauline Cushman, caught spying for the Yankees, was sentenced to hang and was rescued just in time by Union troops. Elizabeth Van Lew hid escaped Union prisoners in her Richmond home, sent messages North in baskets of produce, and planted a servant in Jefferson Davis's home.

tle. Newspapers and politicians urged the army to move on the South. "Forward to Richmond!" they cried. Brigadier General Irvin McDowell was given command of the Northern troops camped in Washington. Lincoln encouraged him to strike, telling him, "You are green; the Rebels are green. You are all green alike." Green or not, the armies soon faced each other across a battlefield on a hot July day.

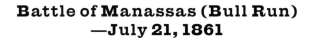

Battle of Manassas (Bull Run) —July 21, 1861

General Irvin McDowell marched 35,000 Northern troops from Washington toward opponent General Pierre Beauregard's 23,000 men. McDowell's Union army looked magnificent. Silk regimental flags waved in the breeze, and the new uniforms were bright and colorful. The soldiers, however, weren't very disciplined. Many broke from the ranks to pick blackberries or to get a drink of water from a stream. Beauregard knew the Northern army was coming. Confederate spy Rose Greenhow sent word to him of the Union plans. The Confederates had just enough time to send for reinforcements for the battle.

Beauregard's troops lined up along winding Bull Run Creek. McDowell ordered his men to cross the creek upstream from the Rebel army and come down hard on their left side, or "flank." The two armies clashed and fought furiously, untrained and frightened though they were. It looked as if the Union troops would break through the Confederate line.

Just as that line began to weaken, a Southern commander spotted General Thomas J. Jackson holding his Virginian troops against the Union forces. "There is Jackson standing like a stone wall!" he cried, hoping to inspire his men to do the same, "Rally behind the Virginians!" The Confederates rallied, attacking the Northerners savagely while howling their "Rebel yell." They yelped and yipped at the top of their lungs. The howl terrified their opponents! Soon the Confederates were joined by reinforcements. To make matters even worse for the Union soldiers, some of the Rebels were dressed in blue. As the Northerners held their fire for troops they thought were their own, the Rebels attacked. The Union troops collapsed.

The inexperienced Union soldiers rushed back toward Washington. In their retreat, they ran into hundreds of civilians who had come out in carriages to witness the battle. Many had even brought picnic lunches! The panicking citizens raced back to the city. The road became a tangle of troops, horses, and civilians in carriages.

The loss shocked the once optimistic Northerners. They thought that one battle would end the war, but now they realized a long struggle lay ahead. Southerners were overjoyed by the victory, but both sides mourned the losses of this first battle. Nearly 2,900 Union men and 1,900 Confederates were killed, wounded, or missing. It seemed to be so many, and yet these numbers would look small in comparison to the losses in the years ahead.

Naming Civil War Battles

Civil War battles sometimes have two names. Southerners often named battles for nearby towns; Northerners named them for landmarks. Bull Run was the name of a creek near Washington. Manassas was a town along that creek.

A North Star Safe Quilt

When slaves escaped on the "Underground Railroad," they traveled at night, guided by the North Star. They hid in wagons with false bottoms, while a "conductor" drove them to the next stop. Safe houses posted special signs—a lantern in an upstairs window, or a "safe" quilt hanging on a line. Slaves could hide in secret rooms in these houses until it was safe for them to move on. Levi and Catharine Coffin were Quakers whose home was known as the "Grand Central Station" of the Railroad. These two kind people helped 3,000 fugitive slaves to freedom.

ADULT SUPERVISION IS RECOMMENDED

What you need

8-inch square of cardboard

Scissors

½ yard each of 4 medium-weight 45-inch-wide fabrics

Pins

Thread

Sewing machine

Iron and ironing board

Muslin fabric (or an old sheet), 45 by 45 inches

Polyester quilt batting, 43 by 43 inches

1. Using the cardboard as a template, cut 25 patches from the fabrics.

2. Arrange them on a flat surface, working from the center out, until you have a design that you like. Each row should have five patches.

3. Starting with the top row, place two patches together with front sides facing and pin ½-inch from the edge (see figure 1). Pin the rest of the top row in this way. Sew the patches at the ½-inch seam (see figure 2). Pin and sew the other rows. Iron the seams all to one side.

4. Pin the rows to each other in the same way, sew them together with a ½-inch seam, and press all the seams to one side (see figure 3).

5. Cut out 5 triangular pieces from the leftover fabric. Fold their edges over ½-inch and sew all around their borders. Center them on the quilt top in the shape of a star (see figure 4), then sew them in place.

6. Place the muslin fabric on a flat surface. Center the quilt batting on top. Place the quilt top over the batting, right side up. Smooth the layers out. Fold the edge of the muslin over a ½-inch, then fold it again over the quilt top (see figure 5). Pin all the layers together. Sew around the border (see figure 6).

12

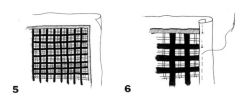

Create a Code

Spies sent messages in code in case they were found by the enemy. Special ciphering squares, like the one to the right, helped them "encipher" (put into code) and decode messages.

Create a secret code sentence. For example, take a famous quote from the Battle of Bull Run.

R A L L Y B E H I N D T H E V I R G I N I A N S R A L L Y B

Write your message below the sentence.

R A L L Y B E H I N D T H E V I R G I N I A N S R A L L Y B
E N E M Y A P P R O A C H I N G Y O U R R I G H T F L A N K

If the message is longer than the code sentence, repeat the code sentence.

To convert your message into code, find the first letter of your message ("E") in the top row of the cipher square. ("Rows" are the letters going across; "columns" are the letters going down.) Locate the first letter of your code sentence ("R") in the first column. Go to the point where these two letters meet (down from "E" and across from "R") to find the cipher letter ("V"). The second letter of the message ("N") and the second letter of the code sentence ("A") meet at "N." The third letters ("E" and "L") meet at "P." The completed enciphered message is:

V N P X W B T W Z B D V O M I O P U C E Z I T Z K F W L L L

The person receiving the message has to know the secret code sentence and have a similar square in order to decipher it. Working backward, they'll find the letter "V" in the row across from "R" and look up to see the first letter of that column, "E."

V N P X W B T W Z B D V O M I O P U C E Z I T Z K F W L L L
R A L L Y B E H I N D T H E V I R G I N I A N S R A L L Y B
E N E M Y A P P R O A C H I N G Y O U R R I G H T F L A N K

Soon they'll read, "Enemy approaching your right flank," and prepare for the fight!

CIPHER SQUARE

```
A B C D E F G H I J K L M N O P Q R S T U V W X Y Z
B C D E F G H I J K L M N O P Q R S T U V W X Y Z A
C D E F G H I J K L M N O P Q R S T U V W X Y Z A B
D E F G H I J K L M N O P Q R S T U V W X Y Z A B C
E F G H I J K L M N O P Q R S T U V W X Y Z A B C D
F G H I J K L M N O P Q R S T U V W X Y Z A B C D E
G H I J K L M N O P Q R S T U V W X Y Z A B C D E F
H I J K L M N O P Q R S T U V W X Y Z A B C D E F G
I J K L M N O P Q R S T U V W X Y Z A B C D E F G H
J K L M N O P Q R S T U V W X Y Z A B C D E F G H I
K L M N O P Q R S T U V W X Y Z A B C D E F G H I J
L M N O P Q R S T U V W X Y Z A B C D E F G H I J K
M N O P Q R S T U V W X Y Z A B C D E F G H I J K L
N O P Q R S T U V W X Y Z A B C D E F G H I J K L M
O P Q R S T U V W X Y Z A B C D E F G H I J K L M N
P Q R S T U V W X Y Z A B C D E F G H I J K L M N O
Q R S T U V W X Y Z A B C D E F G H I J K L M N O P
R S T U V W X Y Z A B C D E F G H I J K L M N O P Q
S T U V W X Y Z A B C D E F G H I J K L M N O P Q R
T U V W X Y Z A B C D E F G H I J K L M N O P Q R S
U V W X Y Z A B C D E F G H I J K L M N O P Q R S T
V W X Y Z A B C D E F G H I J K L M N O P Q R S T U
W X Y Z A B C D E F G H I J K L M N O P Q R S T U V
X Y Z A B C D E F G H I J K L M N O P Q R S T U V W
Y Z A B C D E F G H I J K L M N O P Q R S T U V W X
Z A B C D E F G H I J K L M N O P Q R S T U V W X Y
```

A Soldier's Uniform

Volunteers reported for duty in uniforms of their own design. There were units wearing blue and gray on both sides (causing great confusion in battle), Northerners in bright green, and a group called the Scottish Highlanders who wore kilts. Some copied the French Algerian Zouaves and wore baggy red pants, short blue coats, and red caps with tassels! They were a contrast to some Minnesotans, who dressed like lumberjacks in red flannel shirts and black pants. Eventually, Union soldiers were given uniforms of dark blue coats, light blue pants, and a cap (called a "kepi") with a round, flat crown and a visor. Southerners had similar uniforms with gray jackets and light blue pants. As the war wore on, and supplies became harder to find, the South wore "butternut"—homemade clothes dyed in shades ranging from light brown to dark brown. You can make your own Yankee or Rebel uniform.

ADULT SUPERVISION IS RECOMMENDED

What you need

Old dark blue or gray jacket (check a used clothing store if you can't find one around the house)

Imitation brass buttons

Iron and ironing board

Needle and thread or sewing machine

Yellow ribbon, ¾ to 1 inch in width

Light blue pants

Old baseball cap

Cardboard

Pencil

Scissors

Stapler

(Optional) Fringed sash, broad-brimmed hat, feather, long yellow or white gloves, and boots

1. Take the old jacket and replace the buttons with imitation brass ones. Turn up the lapels and collar of the jacket and iron them flat. With the needle and thread or sewing machine, sew the ribbon down the outside of the pant legs.

2. To make a Union kepi, use the baseball cap as a template to draw a circle on the cardboard with pencil. Then with the scissors cut out the cardboard circle and place it inside the baseball cap. Push it against the top and staple it in place. Make a tuck in the front of the cap so that it bends toward the bill and stitch it down from the inside with needle and thread.

3. If you want to look like a cavalry officer, belt the jacket with a fringed sash and wear a broad-brimmed hat. Add a feather on the side for a dashing look. Cavalrymen also wore long yellow or white gloves (called gauntlets) and boots.

2

Drill, Drill, Drill

fter Bull Run, Northerners knew that a real army would be needed to fight this war. Lincoln removed General Irvin McDowell from command of the Union troops and replaced him with 34-year-old George McClellan. Everyone had high hopes for the young general's success. The newspapers called him a "young Napoleon" and a "man of destiny." His troops called him "Little Mac." McClellan was an engineer who had written books about military tactics. He had served in the Mexican War, and as a civilian became president of a railroad company. McClellan set out to make a trained fighting army of the green volunteers.

When McClellan took command, the Union army was an undisciplined mob. The men wandered the streets of Washington, absent without leave. An excellent organizer and inspiring leader, McClellan brought order and a sense of pride to the 100,000-man force now called the Army of the Potomac. Under his command, a routine was established in the camps, the delivery of supplies organized, and the training of troops was the order of the day—all day.

"Drill, drill, and more drill," was how one soldier described his days. The men were taught to move from "column" (marching formation) into "line" (fighting formation). Orders were barked at them all day long—"Dress to the right!" "Give way to the left!" "Keep well in line!" "Move in quick time! Double-quick!" Regimental bands played military songs. Drummer boys practiced. Bugles rang out, from "reveille" (wake-up) in the morning, to "assembly," "drill," and "taps" at night, letting the soldiers know it was time for lights out.

The army camp began to look like a city. Tents were pitched along streets. Log cabins were built for the officers. Mail was delivered and preachers conducted church services. Supplies were ordered and distributed. Weapons, food, uniforms, knapsacks and mess gear, blankets and tents, wagons, horses, and mules all started to appear. Men lined up for roll call dressed, alert, and proud to be one of Little Mac's soldiers. McClellan reviewed his troops regularly, looking on with satisfaction as the bands played and the men marched.

McClellan organized the three main branches of the army: the infantry, artillery, and cavalry. The infantry fought on foot, its soldiers equipped with small arms. The artillery fought with big guns— cannons and mortars. The cavalry rode on horseback and carried swords. Other departments supported these fighting men. Engineers constructed bridges, forts, and roads; ordnance obtained and maintained weapons; signal and telegraph departments were in charge of sending messages. The soldiers learned to recognize each branch by its insignia, which was

George McClellan

ACTIVITY

Drill Exercises

Line six or more friends in two rows (called "ranks"). Starting at the left of each rank, have your troops alternately call out the numbers one and two. Give the order to "Right face!" The soldiers should turn to their right. All the soldiers who called out "number two!" should take a diagonal step forward and to the right. Now your troops are in column formation, four across, and ready to "forward march," or advance.

On the march, you may see enemy troops ahead. "Double quick" will tell your troops to march briskly to the front. Order them back in line formation by shouting out "Company into line!" The "twos" should step back to where they were and once again your soldiers will form two ranks. In this formation, they are ready to turn and shoot in any direction. They can shoot in a "fire by file" (starting at one end of the line and each firing in turn). They can also volley by rank, in which one rank fires while the second rank reloads.

Who Joined?

Around 900,000 men fought for the South in the Confederate army; 2,100,000 served in the Union army and navy. Young and old jumped at the chance. Farmers, businessmen, laborers and lawyers, professors and planters, new immigrants and men from old established families signed up. After 1863, blacks fought for the Union. Native Americans served on both sides.

Women Soldiers

Hundreds of women cut their hair, took men's names, and fought. Jennie Hodgers, as Albert D. J. Cashire, fought in 40 battles with the 95th Illinois. Kady Brownell fought with a Rhode Island unit and had a song written for her, "The Daughter of the Regiment." Southerner Amy Clark joined up with her husband, and stayed after he was killed.

96th Pennsylvania Infantry Regiment during a drill,
1861

embroidered on their hats. The symbol for infantry was a looped horn; artillery had crossed cannons. The cavalry insignia was a pair of crossed swords, engineers had a castle, and ordnance, a shell and flame.

Each regiment that marched past McClellan flew its own flag, or "colors." On the battlefield, the flags helped soldiers find their units in the smoke and confusion of the fight. They were inscribed with the names of battles the regiments had fought, and carried by the "color-

Johnny Clem

Johnny joined the Union army when he was only nine years old! He tagged along with the 22nd Michigan until the men gave up trying to send him home. When his drum was smashed by a shell during the battle of Shiloh, he received a nickname, "Johnny Shiloh." The soldiers made a shortened rifle for him, which he used to shoot a Rebel officer at Chickamauga. He was captured, exchanged for another prisoner, and returned to the front.

Boy soldier Johnny Clem

bearer." (His was a dangerous job—the enemy always aimed at the man carrying the colors.) Regiments were named for the states they came from and given a number (like 2nd Michigan Cavalry or 151st New York Infantry). This number showed its order among the regiments enrolled from that state. When enough men had enlisted to form a regiment (about 1,000 men) they would close that regiment and then start another regiment with the next number.

Special regiments of "sharpshooters" (skilled riflemen) were usually excused from drill and duty. Sharpshooters practiced shooting all day with their "breech-loading" (loaded from the back) rifles. These riflemen could shoot a plate-sized target at 200 yards—10 times in a row! A special Union regiment of sharpshooters wore dark green uniforms and caps with black ostrich feathers, but even out of uniform they could be recognized, for they often had black eyes from looking through their guns' sights so much.

While the Union soldiers learned how to be an army, the Southerners prepared to fight them. Young men assembled across the South and drilled in village squares. Local craftsmen forged weapons and made shoes for the soldiers while their wives and mothers sewed uniforms and flags. When they left to fight, whole towns came out to wave and cheer. Flags were presented to

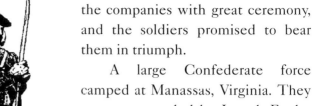

the companies with great ceremony, and the soldiers promised to bear them in triumph.

A large Confederate force camped at Manassas, Virginia. They were commanded by Joseph Eggleston Johnston. An officer in the United States army before secession, Johnston had served on the Western frontier and in Mexico. He had gone to school at West Point with Jefferson Davis. They fought there, over a woman, and their feud still continued even though Johnston was one of the Confederacy's top generals. He had his soldiers build fortifications and place threatening guns along the Potomac River.

Union General George McClellan sent spies to gather information about the movements and size of the enemy army. The spies came back with exaggerated numbers. Even though the Confederate army was only one-fourth the size of McClellan's Army of the Potomac, McClellan believed that he was outnumbered and refused to move against them. He called for more men and provisions. He would make no move until he felt prepared to fight, and it seemed as if that day would never come. Lincoln said the young general had a case of the slows. Though McClellan spoke confidently, his actions were those of a very cautious man. He sent troops to investigate a Confederate camp at Ball's Bluff, 30 miles from Washington.

About the Infantry

100 men = 1 "company" (led by a captain)

10 companies = 1 "regiment" (led by a colonel)

4 regiments = 1 "brigade" (led by a brigadier general)

3 brigades = 1 "division" (led by a major general)

3 divisions (sometimes 4) = 1 corps (led by a major general)

Corps were then combined to make up the "field armies." In the Union there were 16 field armies, often named after rivers (such as the Army of the Potomac). The Confederacy had 23 field armies, usually named after states or parts of the states (such as the Army of Northern Virginia).

About the Artillery

100 men + 6 big guns = 1 battery

5 batteries = 1 battalion

Each big gun had a crew of 8 men. The "gunner" aimed the cannon and gave commands. The others prepared the ammunition and loaded the cannon. Each crew also required a 6-horse team to transport the gun and its "caisson" (ammunition chest) to battle.

About the Cavalry

100 men and horses = 1 company

12 companies = 1 regiment

2 to 5 regiments = 1 brigade

2 to 5 brigades = 1 division

They fell into the hands of the Rebels and many were killed, including a member of the Senate who was a close friend of Lincoln's. This incident made McClellan even more reluctant to enter battle.

One day some Union soldiers realized that one of the Confederate posts had been abandoned. When they investigated, they discovered that what they thought had been a cannon pointed at them was only a log cut to look like a cannon! This discovery was a great embarrassment to the proud General McClellan. Still, he refused to bring his troops against the enemy. The Army of the Potomac would go into winter quarters that year without a fight.

ACTIVITY

A Coffee Can Drum

Eighteen was the minimum age for enlistment, but thousands of boys lied about their age to join. Many were drummers. Their drumbeats communicated orders to the troops. A certain drumbeat called men to drill. The "long roll" was a signal to march into battle. "Rally" ordered scattered forces to regroup, and there was a drum signal for "retreat." These drummer boys also gathered wood, helped set up camp, cooked, and tended the wounded.

What you need

Newspaper

White glue

Coffee can (2-pound size or larger)

¼ yard of heavy acetate cloth

Rubber bands

Scissors

Water

Paper cup

Old paintbrush

Construction paper

Paints or colored markers

2 chopsticks

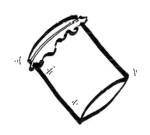

1. Spread newspaper over your workspace.

2. Spread glue around the outside edge of the top of the coffee can. Fit the acetate cloth over the top of the can, pull it down tightly, and stretch rubber bands around it to hold it in place. Let dry for an hour. Using scissors, trim off the extra cloth.

3. Mix 3 tablespoons of glue with 1 tablespoon of water in the paper cup. Paint the mixture over the acetate cloth. Let dry for an hour. Add another coat and let dry for another hour.

4. Cut construction paper to fit around the sides of the coffee can and use paints or colored markers to decorate it. Wrap it around the can and glue into place.

5. Clean the paintbrush immediately and dispose of any extra glue mix in the garbage. Don't pour it down the sink!

6. Use wooden chopsticks as your drumsticks.

21

3
Battles West and East

Union General George McClellan's reports remained the same, "All quiet along the Potomac," but things were far from quiet in the West. To prevent a Union invasion, Confederate troops occupied towns across the border states of Kentucky and Tennessee. They were led by General Albert Sidney Johnston, thought by some to be the best general in the Confederacy. Johnston ordered construction of Fort Henry on the

Tennessee River, and Fort Donelson on the Cumberland, to stop the Union army from advancing. These forts could not withstand the force brought against them by Brigadier General Ulysses S. Grant.

Grant's successes sent a wave of joy across the North. Northerners were also thrilled by a victory at Pea Ridge, Arkansas. A two-day battle there discouraged Confederate troops from attempting to take Missouri.

Ulysses S. Grant

———◆———

He tried farming, sold firewood, worked as a bill collector and as a clerk, but it seemed as if Ulysses S. Grant couldn't succeed at anything. He graduated from West Point, served in the Mexican War, then resigned from the army. Until the Civil War began, he barely scraped together a living. He rejoined the service, eventually to command the entire Union army. Grant conquered Fort Henry, then Fort Donelson.

He demanded of the latter fort's commander "unconditional and immediate surrender." This statement was printed in Northern newspapers, and people joked that Grant's initials stood for "Unconditional Surrender." Actually, his real name was Hiram Ulysses. When he registered at West Point a clerk mistakenly wrote his name as Ulysses Simpson, and the uncomplaining Grant never corrected the error. He was single-minded, quiet, and intense. One soldier said he always looked as if he was determined to "drive his head through a brick wall." He cared little for fanfare and ceremony. His uniform was often dusty and wrinkled. Grant adored his wife, Julia, and their four children. He loved horses, and punished anyone who was cruel to them.

Ulysses S. Grant

Battle of Shiloh—April 6 through 7, 1862

With the forts taken, Confederate General Albert Sidney Johnston ordered his 40,000 troops to gather at Corinth, Mississippi. Union General Ulysses S. Grant took 45,000 men in boats up the Tennessee River to a landing north of Corinth. Here he would join with 25,000 reinforcements and march to Corinth to engage Johnston's army in battle. Grant's Union soldiers landed and camped in the fields and orchards near the country church of Shiloh. As they bedded down that night they could smell the sweet fragrance of peach trees in bloom.

Johnston learned of the Union movements and decided to destroy Grant's army before it was reinforced. Though his officers pleaded with him to hold back, Johnston was determined to go to battle. "We will attack at daylight," he said, "Tomorrow at twelve o'clock, we will water our horses in the Tennessee River."

As the sun rose, a Union patrol ran into an advance Confederate brigade in the woods near their camp. Shots rang out and the battle of Shiloh began. The Union soldiers had been preparing breakfast, and were taken completely by surprise when the Rebels poured into their camps. They left their campfires and scrambled for their guns. They were quickly driven back by the assault. As the Rebel soldiers moved forward, they stopped long enough to sample some Yankee breakfast!

The first attacked were Ohio men led by Union General William Tecumseh Sherman.

KEY
- City
- ☆ Battle Site

☆ **Shiloh**

● Memphis

M I S S I S S I P P I

A L A B A M A

MISSISSIPPI RIVER

☆ **Jackson**

☆ **Vicksburg**

L O U I S I A N A

Mobile Bay

New Orleans

Map of Mississippi, Louisiana, and Tennessee showing some of the battles fought in these states.

Though they were taken by surprise, Sherman's courage in the face of the battering assault helped them hold the line. Sherman was wounded twice that day, and three of his horses were killed as he rode them in battle.

Men fought and fell along a battle front nearly three miles long. Peach blossoms fluttered to the ground when the trees were struck by bullets. The Union troops fell back. Many fled for the river and some tried to swim across it to escape.

One Union division held its ground behind a sunken road. Grant ordered them to hold that position "at all hazards" and called the remaining troops to set up a line of defense behind them near the Tennessee River. The assault on the men at the sunken road was so fierce that survivors later named it the "Hornets' Nest." The Confederate fire was ceaseless. One soldier described it as a "never-ending, terrible roar." The small group of Union soldiers held their position for six hours against twelve assaults and all of the cannons of the Confederates.

Near the sunken road, battle raged in the peach orchard. As Confederate General Albert Sidney Johnston shouted to his men to follow him in battle, he was shot in the leg. He swayed in his saddle, blood filling his boot. Johnston, as commander, would normally have had a personal physician at his side but he had sent his doctor away to tend to wounded prisoners. Without medical care, the great leader died.

His was not the only blood flowing that day.

William Tecumseh Sherman

Sherman was head of the Louisiana Military Academy when the Civil War broke out. He left this Southern military academy to join the Union soldiers, though he had many friends in the Southern states. Sherman was orphaned at age nine. He was educated at West Point and had been a banker in California. In his letters during the war, Sherman drew entertaining sketches for his eight children. A tall, thin redhead, Sherman was intense, tough, and shrewd. He was called "Cump" or "Uncle Billy." Newspapers said he was crazy when he predicted the war would be a long struggle.

What's In a Name?

Shiloh is a Hebrew word meaning "Place of Peace."

William Tecumseh Sherman

So many wounded men and horses, suffering from thirst, crawled to a shallow pond to drink that their blood colored the water red and the lake was renamed the Bloody Pond. The Rebels had pushed their enemies nearly all the way to the river, to Grant's last line of defense. There the day ended, with Union gunboats on the river firing on the Rebel army, who fell back as night came on.

During the night, 25,000 Union reinforcements arrived to fill Grant's ranks. At daybreak, the larger Union army attacked the Confederate troops. By the end of the day they recaptured the field of battle, and the Confederates marched in retreat.

It proved a costly victory for the North. There were shocking losses on both sides, with more than 23,000 killed, wounded, or captured. There were more casualties in the two-day battle than in all of the wars Americans had fought in up to that time combined. Western Tennessee was now in Northern hands, and the Confederacy lost an important commander.

While the armies fought at Shiloh, combined Union army and navy assaults took forts along the Mississippi River. Later that month, David Farragut ran a fleet of warships past the batteries of Forts Jackson and St. Philip at the mouth of the Mississippi River. With cannons blasting and his flagship on fire, he steamed past the forts and captured New Orleans. In June, citizens of Memphis watched from the banks of the Mississippi River as a great battle raged between Union ironclads and a Rebel fleet armored with

Lincoln's Rebel Relatives and Other Families Divided by War

President Abraham Lincoln's wife, Mary Todd, had family fighting for the Confederate cause. Mary's half-brother Samuel died at Shiloh, fighting for the South. She had one brother and three half-brothers in the Confederate army, along with three of her sisters' husbands. One was killed in Baton Rouge and another at Chickamauga.

A senator from Kentucky had two sons who became generals—one in the Confederate army and one in the Union. A Union general had three brothers who fought for the Confederacy. One time a Yankee soldier captured a Rebel only to find that his prisoner was his own brother! Another Union soldier spotted his brother in a line of captured Confederate prisoners and stopped to shake his hand. "What are you doing in such bad company?" he asked.

The Battle of Shiloh
BY THURE DE THULSTRUP

bales of cotton. To the dismay of the townspeople, seven of their eight ships were sunk or captured, and Memphis became an occupied city. The Union now held the mouth and the northern reaches of the Mississippi River, a critical water route for trade and troop transport.

In the East, President Lincoln was frustrated with his commanding general. No matter what he suggested or how much he urged him, McClellan wouldn't move against the enemy.

Battle of the Monitor and the Virginia— March 9, 1862

Union sailors guarding Hampton Roads, Virginia, in March of 1861 had heard rumors about an attack, but nothing prepared them for the sight of the C.S.S. *Virginia*. Looking like "the roof of a very big barn belching smoke," the ship was a new invention— an "ironclad."

The Confederates had refitted a captured Union ship (the U.S.S. *Merrimack*) with 4 inches of iron plating, 10 guns, and a 1,500-pound cast-iron ram. They renamed it the *Virginia*. Shots slid right off her iron sides. The *Virginia* sank one wooden enemy ship, set another on fire, and crippled a third before a Union ship, the U.S.S. *Monitor*, arrived.

Now, the Confederate sailors were shocked. The *Monitor* was flat-bottomed like a raft, built to maneuver in shallow waters. It, too, was covered with layers of iron. It had two guns in a revolving turret and a fortified pilot house with eye slits all around it. The sailors said it looked like a tin can on a shingle.

The *Virginia*'s shells exploded harmlessly on the *Monitor*'s sides. The ships circled, firing, until the *Virginia*'s pilot house was damaged. Then the *Virginia* got stuck on the river bottom. Her sailors freed her, only to find they were running out of powder. With the tide going out and little ammunition left, the *Virginia* left for deeper water. The battle was over. Neither side won, but both now knew that wooden-hulled ships were obsolete. After this battle, both sides hurried to produce fleets of ironclads.

28

Boy sailor, called a "powder monkey"

David Glasgow Farragut

David went to sea when he was only nine years old! It wasn't unusual for kids to work aboard ships, especially if their fathers were seafaring men. Sailors nicknamed these young sailors "powder monkeys."

When the Civil War broke out, David Farragut was in his sixties. Union navy officers were reluctant to give him a command because he was from Virginia and, they thought, too old. Farragut proved them wrong. He was against secession and more vigorous than many men half his age. He celebrated his birthdays with a handspring and refused to consider himself old until he couldn't do one anymore. He was given command of a fleet and sent to the Gulf of Mexico. The capture of New Orleans proved his worth to the Union.

Admiral David Glasgow Farragut

According to McClellan, there were never enough troops or supplies, the weather was always bad, and for a while the young Union general was in bed with typhoid fever. He became the subject of a popular song, "What Are You Waiting For, Tardy George?" Lincoln grew impatient and suggested that if McClellan did not want to use the army, he might borrow it himself for a while.

McClellan finally got underway in March. The Union army moved down the Virginia coast in a great fleet of barges carrying men, horses, guns, and supplies. McClellan planned to bring the army up the peninsula of the James River to attack Richmond, Virginia. He thought if he could capture this Confederate capital, the war would be won. Once there, he became nervous. Lincoln had insisted he leave some troops behind to guard Washington, and McClellan wished he had them along, still convinced the Rebel army far outnumbered his own. Actually, the opposite was true. The Union troops approaching Richmond had nearly three times the number of Confederates protecting it.

The Rebels made up for their numbers with strategy. A Confederate major general named John Magruder held the end of the peninsula. Magruder knew he couldn't risk a fight against the large Union army in front of him, so he staged a drama instead. He shifted his artillery around so it seemed as if he had a great number of weapons. He marched columns of men along a road, then circled them back to march it again so it would

The Anaconda Plan

The Union Navy's actions along the Mississippi River were part of the Anaconda Plan. Lincoln ordered ships to blockade the 3,500 miles of Confederate coastline so Confederate ships would be prevented from leaving or entering Southern ports. The goal was that, eventually, the South would be unable to trade with any other countries, and would run out of supplies. It would be held in a stranglehold, like that of an anaconda snake around its prey. The South built sleek, fast ships to outrun those of the Union navy. Southern captains slipped out of harbors on moonless nights to sail for Cuba or Nassau and trade cotton for necessities and luxuries.

Union sailors spent long hours on the lookout for blockade runners. They swabbed the decks and shined brass, fished, played music, wrote home, or read. They ate preserved beef, which they called "salt horse," and "dogs' bodies" (dried peas boiled in a cloth bag). They rose at five in the morning to report for duty and drill. They took turns standing watch. Saturdays were "make and mend" days. Their clothes were inspected and, if found unfit, thrown overboard! On Sundays, the whole ship was inspected. The men were always glad to fall back into their hammocks at night. When a blockade-runner was spotted, all hands ran to their posts and full sails and steam were put on to capture the enemy ship. The Union navy couldn't capture all the runners but it eventually tightened the blockade around the South and made it very difficult for the Confederacy to get much-needed supplies.

National Archives

Thomas Jonathan "Stonewall" Jackson

Thomas J. "Stonewall" Jackson

Stonewall Jackson was one of the South's greatest generals, and a most eccentric man. This West Point graduate served in the Mexican War, then taught at the Virginia Military Institute. He was secretive, ambitious, fearless, and deeply religious. He cared nothing for casualties, and drove his men until they dropped. They called him "Old Blue Light," because of the way his blue eyes lit up when he rode into battle. He rode his horse with his left arm raised high above his head and always wore an old rumpled coat from his Mexican War days. He ate lemons and raw onions (but never pepper—he claimed it made his left leg ache), then drank buttermilk for his upset stomach.

Robert E. Lee

Lincoln asked Robert E. Lee to command the Northern army, but Lee chose to fight on the side of his beloved state of Virginia. His father, Henry "Light Horse Harry" Lee, a Revolutionary War hero, squandered the family fortune and left his family when Robert was young. Robert E. Lee graduated from West Point second in his class and had a distinguished military career. He married Mary Custis, a granddaughter of George Washington's wife Martha, and they had seven children. When the Civil War broke out, he was superintendent of West Point. Lee was a brilliant and courageous general who took risks others wouldn't dare. Tall and handsome, with gray hair and beard, he looked magnificent on his gray horse, Traveller. He was honest, considerate, and a gentleman in every way. His soldiers called him "Marse Robert." He believed in them, and they returned his trust and were entirely devoted to their general. Lee was one of the greatest military commanders in history. Eventually he became commander-in-chief of all of the Confederate troops.

Robert E. Lee

seem like a huge force. McClellan, convinced that he faced one of the biggest armies of all time, settled in for a long siege.

Just as McClellan had his troops dug in, the Rebels pulled back. The Union troops followed them. They clashed, then the Rebels pulled back again. This time the Union army followed them to the gates of Richmond, but McClellan was reluctant to attack the city until he had all of his army.

Confederate commanders made a plan to be certain McClellan didn't receive those reinforcements. General Thomas J. Jackson, called "Stonewall" ever since his brave stand at Manassas, created a diversion. He went north and led a brilliant campaign in Virginia's Shenandoah Valley.

Jackson's presence in the Shenandoah Valley was so close to Washington, it made Northern leaders very nervous. Lincoln sent 55,000 troops to meet him. Jackson moved his men from one end of the valley to another, capturing enemy supplies, striking in unexpected rear-guard actions, and confounding the enemy in every way. He marched his men at an impossible pace. They moved so quickly they called themselves "foot cavalry." Stonewall Jackson and his army, outnumbered four to one, marched 350 miles, faced three enemy forces, and won five battles, all while keeping Union troops from going to McClellan's aid. Finally, he was called back to join the Confederate commander Joseph Johnston and his army outside of Richmond, Virginia.

The Battle of Seven Pines began before his arrival. McClellan's troops were so close to Richmond they could hear bells tolling in the city. Confederate General Joseph Johnston sent his men against the Northern army, but delays and miscommunications haunted the Southerners all that day. Toward dusk, hoping to correct these mistakes, Johnston rode out to the field to meet with his commanders. He was hit in the shoulder and fell, wounded. He refused to let his men carry him off the field until they retrieved his sword. His father had carried that sword in the Revolutionary War. The proud Johnston would rather have died than leave it behind. The day ended with no gains made by either side in the battle, but another Confederate leader had fallen.

Confederate President Jefferson Davis and his military advisor Robert E. Lee rode out to the battlefield that day. With the enemy so near to Richmond and the commander of the army badly wounded, Davis turned to his trusted advisor for leadership. Lee became commander of the force he would rename the "Army of Northern Virginia."

4

Camp Life

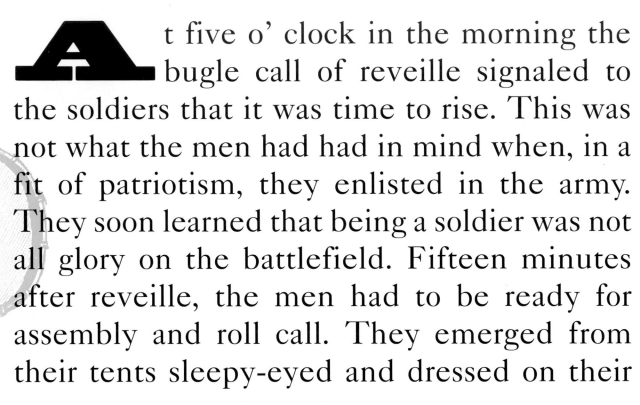

At five o' clock in the morning the bugle call of reveille signaled to the soldiers that it was time to rise. This was not what the men had had in mind when, in a fit of patriotism, they enlisted in the army. They soon learned that being a soldier was not all glory on the battlefield. Fifteen minutes after reveille, the men had to be ready for assembly and roll call. They emerged from their tents sleepy-eyed and dressed on their

way to the assembly ground. After roll call, they received their orders for the day, such as cleaning up after the horses or chopping firewood. Others unloaded supply wagons or were assigned to sentry duty. Everyone else had to drill.

Artillerymen had to learn how to shoot the big guns. These included cannons, such as "siege guns" with long barrels that could blast through walls at a long range; "mortars," which

were short and stubby, fired at a slow speed, and were used to lob shells into fortifications; and "howitzers," mid-range cannons with medium-length barrels. The cannons were described by the number of inches in their bore diameters (such as the "3-inch ordnance rifle") or by the weight of their projectiles (the "12-pounder Napoleon"). They fired "shot" (solid balls of iron); shells (iron balls filled with explosive

Ballads of the Battlefields

All Quiet Along the Potomac Tonight

The Battle Cry of Freedom

The Battle Hymn of the Republic

Dixie

The Girl I Left Behind

Home Sweet Home

John Brown's Body

Just Before the Battle, Mother

My Old Kentucky Home

Tenting Tonight on the Old Campground

The Yellow Rose of Texas

Reveille on a Winter Morning
BY HENRY BACON

charges); "spherical case" (shells filled with powder and musket balls); or "canister" (tin cans filled with iron balls).

Infantrymen practiced with their rifles or rifle-muskets, including the Springfield, a single-shot muzzle-loader; the Enfield, the weapon most commonly used by Southern soldiers; or dozens of other types of long arms, from flintlock muskets to Spencer rifles. The newly invented rifle-musket had "rifling," or curved grooves, inside the barrels, which caused bullets to spin.

35

*Engineers of the 8th
New York State Militia,*
1861

Its bullet was a cone-shaped lead projectile called a "minié ball," named after Minié, its inventor. On firing, its base expanded, forcing it to follow the grooves of the rifle's barrel. The minié ball traveled five times farther than the old musket ball and hit its target with much greater accuracy.

To fire, the soldiers had to load their muskets with powder and minié ball, tamp them down with a ramrod, and replace a percussion cap. It was very difficult to do all of this in the face of enemy fire, but with practice a soldier could shoot three rounds in a minute. A bayonet was fitted onto the end of the gun's muzzle, but though the soldiers practiced the steps and lunges of bayonet drill, they rarely used the bayonet in battle. More often it served as a candle holder, tent stake, or shovel.

Sharpshooters took aim with a British Whitworth or a Sharp's Rifle, rifles that could shoot accurately at 1,000 yards. Cavalrymen used sabers, "carbines" (light, short-barreled rifles),

ACTIVITY

Berry Ink

In the South, there was a shortage of ink and paper, but the Confederate soldiers found a way around the problem. They made ink from the juice of berries and used goose quills or cornstalks as pens. They wrote their replies on the letters they received from home, writing between the lines of the old letter, and they made makeshift envelopes from old letters, too.

What you need

¼ cup raspberries or strawberries

¼ teaspoon vinegar

Soup or cereal bowl

Spoon

Scissors

A bird's feather

Paper

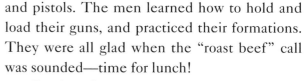

Place berries and vinegar in the bowl. Crush the berries with the back of the spoon until you have a smooth liquid. This is your ink. Now use the scissors to snip the tip off the shaft of the feather on an angle. You now have a quill pen. Using your paper, try to write a letter with the quill pen and berry ink. Feel what it was like for a Civil War soldier to write a letter home.

and pistols. The men learned how to hold and load their guns, and practiced their formations. They were all glad when the "roast beef" call was sounded—time for lunch!

In the afternoon, the soldiers tended to housekeeping chores. They cleaned their guns and shoes and sewed patches on their uniforms. They washed their clothes in streams or in logs that had been scooped out to make basins. Once a week, all the packs were laid out and tents straightened for inspection. With the chores done, the men sat outside their tents to whittle and tell jokes and tall tales to one another. There was always someone to challenge to a game of checkers or chess or cards. Some of the fellows played a new game called baseball. If it was wintertime, they organized into armies and had giant snowball fights. Off in one corner of the camp a group might rehearse a play to perform for the others later that night. Others organized brass bands and choirs, and put on concerts.

Many spent their afternoons writing. Most of the soldiers were away from home for the first time, and felt homesick. Writing letters helped them feel they were still part of the lives of their families and friends. The soldiers kept diaries, too. In some camps, if they stayed long enough, the soldiers set up lending libraries and shared popular novels such as *The Count of Monte Cristo* and *Ivanhoe*. They exchanged magazines and newspapers. They published their own camp newspapers. Everyone's favorite reading, though, remained letters from home. Mail call was the highlight of the day. Letters from family, friends,

Soldiers in front of their wooden hut, "Pine Cottage"

Less serious were the horse and foot races held in camp. Some even held lice races! Lice were a real annoyance in the camps, but the soldiers found one way to make light of the problem. They would place the lice on plates and hold races to see which one could cross its plate first! One soldier won every time. His friends, suspecting a trick, found out that he got his lice to run faster by heating his plate before the race.

In the late afternoon they would reassemble for inspection and a dress parade, followed by supper. Soldiers North and South found plenty to grumble about at mealtimes. The preserved meat they were given was so bad the soldiers called it "embalmed beef." They would pretend it was a dead body and give it a funeral! Afterward they would risk stealing a chicken or a hog from a local farm for their meal. They would roast the meat on a stick over the fire, set out their tin plates and utensils, and feel as if they had a feast fit for a king.

Other rations included salt pork, dried apples, beans, and rice. Union soldiers got something called "desiccated" vegetables. These were cubes of dried vegetables that had to be soaked for hours until they became "sort of edible." They looked like they contained carrots, turnips, and parsnips but tasted most like straw. The soldiers hated them and called them "desecrated" vegetables. When they couldn't stand another meal of straw they would head for "Robbers' Row." This was what they called the line of "sutlers" tents (merchants who followed

and sweethearts were read, reread, and cherished. Some lucky soldiers would get care packages, boxes from home full of gifts such as food, socks, needles and thread, and paper.

There were camp barbers, camp postmen, and camp churches. Photographers set up studios in wagons and the men stood in long lines to get their photographs taken. They sent them home on little cards called "cartes-de-visite." Usually the photograph would show the soldier posing in a very serious and heroic stance.

There's a spot that the soldiers all love; the mess tent is the place that we mean. And the dish that we like to see there is the old-fashioned white Army bean.

—A FAVORITE SOLDIERS' TUNE

National Archives

4th Michigan Infantry band

the troops and sold them supplies). The sutlers' displays of canned fruits and vegetables, butter, cheese, cakes, and pies made the soldiers' mouths water. The soldiers' pay (a Union soldier received $13 a month in 1861; a Confederate, slightly less) didn't allow them to buy from the sutler very often.

The Confederate soldier had to make do on much less. His rations generally included either beef or pork, cornmeal, peas, and rice. As the war went on, it became more and more difficult to find supplies for the troops. Their uniforms grew ragged, and they depended on captured Union guns and supply trains for their own supplies. Shoes were scarce. Later in the war, men on both sides had to tighten their belts.

In the summertime, the soldiers made their homes in tents. In the Northern army, the "Sibley tent" was commonly used. Named for Henry Sibley, who had explored in the West, it looked like the tepees of the Indians he saw there. It was a large tent (18 feet around and 12 feet high) with a large pole in the center and covered with canvas. At the top, a circular opening one foot in diameter provided ventilation. The Sibley was meant to hold 12 men, but sometimes as many as 20 slept in one. There was a lot of

Play the Bones

If a soldier didn't have a musical instrument to play, he could easily make one from that day's dinner.

What you need

2 bones from a rib dinner, washed clean and dried, or 2 teaspoons

To play the bones, cup one of them in your hand and hit it with the other, rhythmically. You can also hold them (or the teaspoons) in one hand, one between your middle and index fingers and one between your index finger and your thumb. Shake your hand to tap out a rhythm. With practice, it will sound like you're playing castanets.

grumbling and fighting over space and blankets. The occupants of the tents made an agreement: they would all go to sleep facing the same direction and if, during the night, one man woke up and wanted to turn over, he had to give a warning. He'd wake the others up, give the command for a right or left turn, and the whole group would turn over at once! Shortly after the start of the war, the two-man "Tente d' Abri" was introduced. The men quickly nicknamed it a "dog tent," because, they said, it was only comfortable enough to accommodate a dog—and a small one at that!

For long sieges and during the winter, the men built log cabins. A winter camp looked just like a small town. The soldiers built huts of wooden logs with fireplaces of stone and mud and whatever bricks they could salvage. They named their cabins after fancy hotels, calling them "The Parker House" or "The Willard Hotel," or they would put up a more descriptive sign like "The Hole in the Wall" or "The Swine Hotel."

A box for a chair and a barrel table suited the soldiers just fine. Grain sacks were turned into hammocks. After months and years of soldiering, some men found that they were perfectly comfortable sitting on the floor or sleeping on the ground. In fact, many soldiers found it hard to get used to furniture and soft beds when they returned home from the war.

In the evening, at half past eight, they would assemble again for roll call. After that, there was a little free time to socialize and loaf around. When it grew dark, the soldiers built campfires and sat near the warm flames in the night, amusing each other with stories, jokes, and songs. Sometimes a soldier would bring a precious fiddle out from his tent. Another would pull a jaw harp out of his pocket. Others played the bones, striking them together in rhythm. The music inspired some energetic jigs and dances around the fire. As the night wore on, the soldiers sang lonesome songs about the sweethearts they had left behind.

At the end of the day, in their tents or cabins, some soldiers would read, some would write, some would pray by the light of a single candle stuck on a bayonet. As the bugle called taps for lights out, many lay awake wondering what the next day would bring.

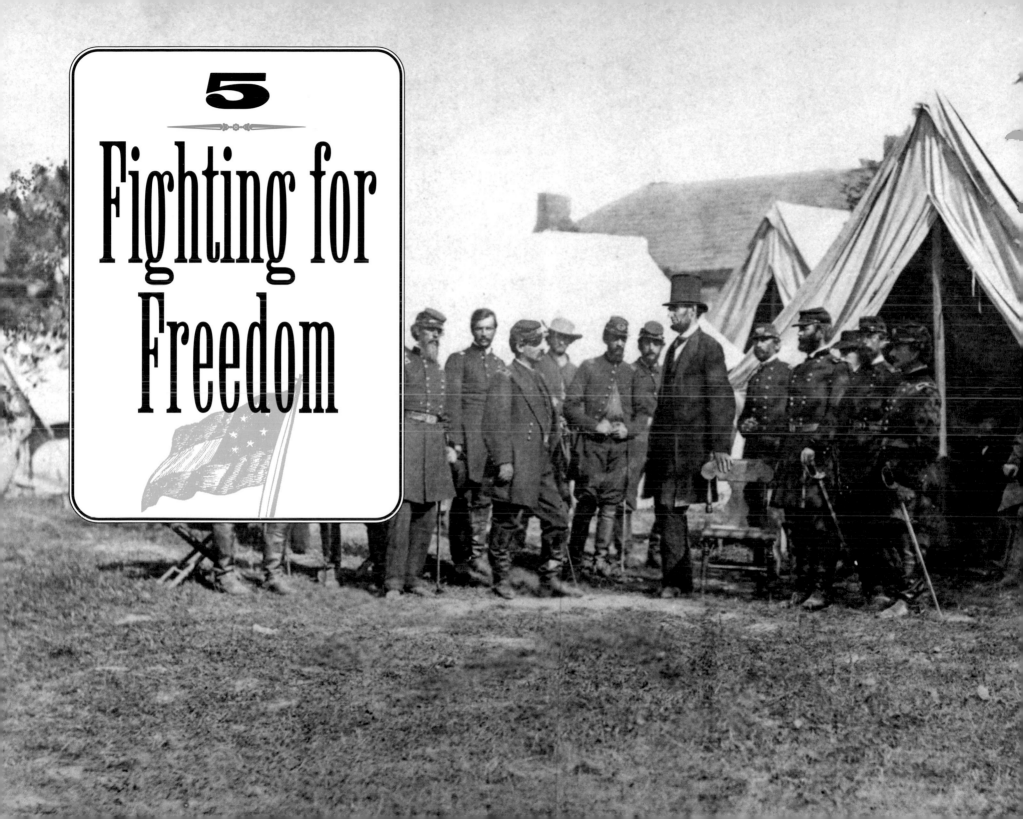

5
Fighting for Freedom

eneral Robert E. Lee faced a desperate situation, as Union troops only five short miles away threatened Richmond and Lee's army. He met the challenge. He reorganized his troops and set them to work fortifying the city. He sent his cavalry leader, Jeb Stuart, with 1,200 of his riders to gather information on the enemy. Then he made a plan.

In four days, Stuart rode all the way around the Army of the Potomac. With the enemy in pursuit, Stuart's cavalry skirmished, destroyed Union supplies, and captured horses. As he and his men neared the end of their dangerous loop, they crossed a river and destroyed the bridge behind them with the Union soldiers hot on their heels. One of the Yankee cavalrymen pursuing Stuart was his wife's father!

Stuart reported to Robert E. Lee that Union General George McClellan had 60,000 men on the south bank of the Chickahominy River, and 30,000 guarding a supply base north of it. Lee decided to attack the smaller force. He hoped to destroy them and cut the rest of the Union army off from their supplies. He sent for Stonewall Jackson, instructing him to flank the Union troops and attack from the rear. Lee ordered three other divisions to attack from the front at the same time. To be sure that McClellan, who was with the larger force, didn't join the fight, John Magruder was once again assigned to play-act for

James E. B. "Jeb" Stuart

Jeb Stuart was a young and dashing cavalryman who liked nothing better than adventure and glory. He looked the part, with his knee-high boots and long gloves, red-lined cape and yellow sash. The bearded, blue-eyed Stuart also wore an ostrich feather pinned to the side of his felt hat. Stuart had ridden in the U.S. cavalry before the war, then served the Confederacy until his death in May of 1864.

Portrait of James Ewell Brown "Jeb" Stuart

him. Magruder had his men march up and down in front of McClellan's army and call out orders to imaginary troops. He fooled McClellan once more. For the next seven days, the Confederate army slammed into the Union troops.

The Seven Days' Battles— June 26 through July 2, 1862

The weeklong battle moved from town to town as the armies manuevered for position. At Mechanicsville, Lee sent Confederate commander Ambrose Powell Hill forward. Hill, who always wore a red shirt on days of battle, put on his battle shirt and led his men in a fierce attack. They fought valiantly against heavy Union fire until the sun went down. The fight was renewed at Gaines' Mill, where the Yankees stubbornly held off their attackers for hours. The Southerners won the day when a fierce brigade from Texas, led by John Bell Hood, ran howling against the Union center and sent the enemy scattering.

Union General McClellan began to withdraw his army. At the town of Savage's Station, John Magruder attacked the Union rear guard as it withdrew. As darkness fell, a storm broke and the fighting ended with no advantage to either side. The battle picked up again at Frayser's Farm, beginning late the next day and lasting until long after dark. In the brutal hand-to-hand struggle, the soldiers fought with bayonets and the butt-ends of muskets. The Seven Days ended on Malvern Hill on the James River, with

**I shall do my best to save the army.
Send more gunboats.**

—GEORGE MCCLELLAN FROM MALVERN HILL

Spying from the Air

Union General George McClellan sent a hot air balloon up in the sky every day to survey the Confederate army's positions. The Rebels greatly enjoyed shooting at the huge balloon as it soared in the sky. One day, it nearly landed in their camp! Later, the Confederacy had a balloon as well, made of the donated silk dresses of patriotic Southern ladies.

National Archives

Balloon Ascension,
1862

the Union army fortified by its gunboats. The Southerners advanced while the Union guns blazed. With darkness the fighting ended, and so did the Seven Days.

When the sun rose after the last day, the field of battle was a terrible sight. North and South buried their dead and carried the wounded to camp. Union casualties were close to 10,000. The Confederates lost more than 16,000. It was a hard-won fight, but Lee had driven the invading army away from Richmond. Two days later, on the fourth of July, soldiers from both sides picked berries together in the fields and traded stories about the fight.

The attack on Richmond had failed. Lincoln called McClellan and his army back to the North and placed McClellan's forces under the command of Major General John Pope. Perhaps Pope would have better luck against Richmond—and Robert E. Lee.

This done, Lincoln set his mind on other things. He had always hated slavery and hoped to see the end of it one day. Perhaps the North could win this war to preserve the Union, but what would be the point of sacrificing all those lives in battle if that Union would still be poisoned by slavery? The war was only worth fighting if it ended the terrible institution. Lincoln

decided to give the North a new reason to fight. He would make the war to save the Union a war against slavery.

Lincoln often walked to his War Department's telegraph office late at night. He liked to see the messages as they came in from his commanders. He spent the hot nights of that July there, writing a draft of a document to free the slaves—an emancipation proclamation. He wrote it slowly and carefully, and each night when it was time to go home, he locked it away in a desk.

Second Manassas (Second Bull Run)—August 29 through 30, 1862

The Confederate leader, General Robert E. Lee, stayed awake late on those hot nights, too. He wasn't about to wait to be attacked. Leaving a small force to defend Richmond, Lee moved his troops to meet Major General Pope's. He sent Stonewall Jackson ahead with 12,000 men. They clashed with advance divisions of Pope's army at the Battle of Cedar Mountain. At first, the smaller but forceful Northern army had the advantage, but Jackson rallied his men and the Southerners broke through with a fierce coun-

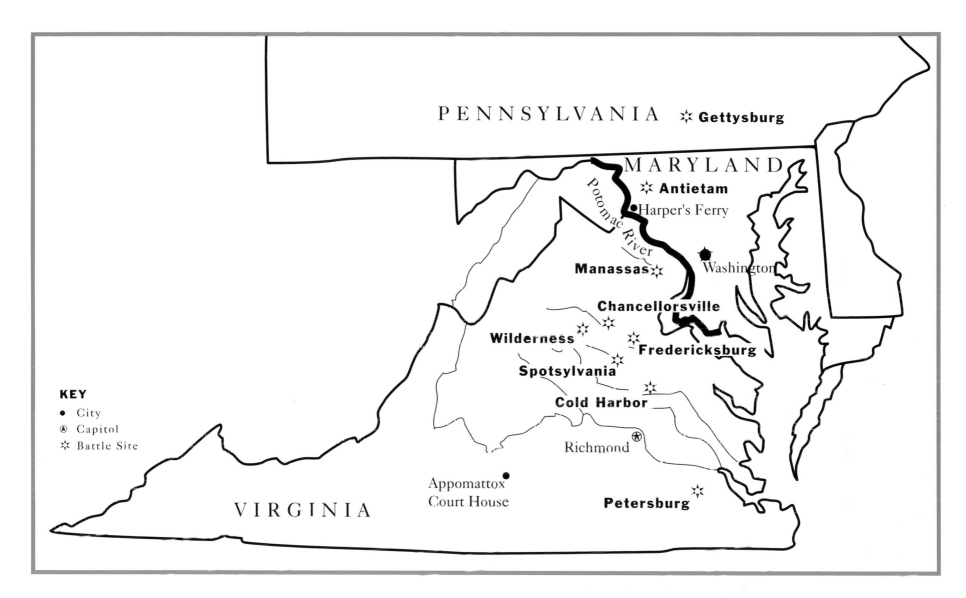

PENNSYLVANIA ☼ **Gettysburg**

M A R Y L A N D

☼ **Antietam**

•Harper's Ferry

Potomac River

•Washington

Manassas☼

Chancellorsville
☼

Wilderness☼

☼ **Fredericksburg**

Spotsylvania
☼

☼

Cold Harbor

Richmond ⊛

KEY
• City
⊛ Capitol
☼ Battle Site

•
Appomattox
Court House

☼
Petersburg

V I R G I N I A

Map of Virginia, Pennsylvania, and Maryland showing
some of the battles fought in these states.

Give my compliments to them, and tell the Stonewall Brigade to maintain her reputation.

—JACKSON'S REPLY TO AN OFFICER'S REQUEST FOR REINFORCEMENTS DURING A DESPERATE FIGHT

Union Scouts Watch as Lee's Troops Cross the Potomac River

BY ALFRED WAUD

terattack. After Union forces fell back, Lee divided his army. Stonewall Jackson marched his men around Pope's lines to Manassas, the Union supply post near the site of the war's first battle. The Southerners plundered the Union supplies, burned everything they couldn't carry away, and disappeared. General Pope was furious! His entire army converged on the region but couldn't find Stonewall Jackson anywhere. Jackson was waiting in a nearby forest for the rest of the Southern army under Robert E. Lee and James Longstreet to join him.

When a Union division unknowingly marched past Jackson's position, Jackson attacked them savagely. John Pope launched repeated assaults the following day and confidently wired Lincoln that he had won a great victory. He spoke too soon. Angry and focused on the enemy before him, Pope failed to listen to warnings that Confederate reinforcements were approaching. James Longstreet and Robert E. Lee came up from behind and crushed the Union army. For the second time in the war, Union troops retreated from Manassas. This time the casualty list was much greater. John Pope was sent off to a post in the West and George McClellan once again was placed in charge.

James Longstreet

The tall, husky Longstreet was one of Robert E. Lee's favorite generals. Lee called him "my old warhorse" and his soldiers called him "Old Pete." Longstreet attended West Point, served in the Mexican War, and eventually commanded half of Lee's army. He was calm and confident, with nerves of steel, and though he dressed in weather-stained clothes and an old black hat, Longstreet had an air of command. He took good care of his men, and received their undying loyalty in return.

James Longstreet

Robert E. Lee didn't want to stop there. He wanted to move the war into the North. He wanted to stay on the heels of the Yankees and wear them down. Perhaps Northern civilians would sicken of war if they saw it in their own land. Perhaps, too, a victory on Northern soil would bring support from European nations. Lee wrote to Confederate President Davis, "We can-not afford to be idle," and took his army across the Potomac River into Maryland.

The citizens of Maryland, used to the well-supplied troops of the Union army, were astonished by the sight of the lean and savage-looking Rebels, laughing and talking as they marched. The men looked very hungry and many of them marched barefoot along the rocky roads. It was obvious, though, that these ragged men were ferocious fighters.

Lee drew up a plan to capture the railroad center of Harrisburg, Pennsylvania. James Longstreet and his men were to lead the way. Confederate General D. H. Hill was assigned to the rear of the army to protect the artillery and supply trains. Stonewall Jackson would remove the Union troops holding the nearby town of Harpers Ferry, then rejoin the others to take Harrisburg. Lee distributed copies of his plan to his commanders. An assistant tucked one copy in his pocket, wrapped around three cigars he looked forward to smoking at camp that night. He thought it might make a nice souvenir of his service in the war.

Unfortunately, he lost his souvenir; the paper fell from his pocket, and the next morning two Union officers found it. They couldn't believe what they'd found! They showed it to their commander and he sent the precious piece of paper to Union headquarters. George McClellan now knew the Confederate army's exact position and plans.

A Confederate alerted General Lee that McClellan had his plans and was on the attack.

Rival Suitors

Before the war, Union General George McClellan and Confederate General Ambrose Powell Hill both had courted the same woman. McClellan married her. Some soldiers thought that made Hill fight especially hard against the enemy.

Union General George McClellan and his military staff during the battle of Antietam
WOODCUT FROM *HARPER'S WEEKLY*

Lee worked fast to ready his men for battle. The town of Sharpsburg, Maryland, was midway between his divided army. He headed there with 18,000 men and positioned them on a ridge above Antietam Creek. "We will make our stand on those hills," he said. He sent word to D. H. Hill to hold the Union troops back for as long as possible. He sent a message to Stonewall Jackson to hurry and join him at Sharpsburg.

At Harpers Ferry, Stonewall Jackson's troops captured 12,000 prisoners and a great supply of weapons. There was no time to sit back and

The 54th Massachusetts

Two of Frederick Douglass's sons joined the all-black 54th Massachusetts Regiment. In July of 1863, after a two-day march, the 54th volunteered to lead an attack on Fort Wagner in South Carolina. Not a man hesitated as they marched into a hail of cannon fire from the fort. Half of them were killed, including the color-bearer. The soldier who retrieved the color-bearer's flag was wounded four times as he brought it back to safety. Frederick Douglass's sons survived the battle. Regimental Colonel Robert Gould Shaw, a white man from a Boston abolitionist family, was buried with his men. His father said "We can imagine no holier place than that in which he is . . . nor wish him better company."

enjoy the victory. They marched to join Lee, leaving Ambrose Powell Hill's division behind to oversee the captured supplies and prisoners. At South Mountain, D. H. Hill and his men held off two Union corps for a full day, giving General Lee precious time to get ready for battle. McClellan showed his usual caution, moving carefully, even though he knew Lee's plans.

The Battle of Antietam— September 17, 1862

The Rebels looking down on Antietam Creek were very nervous as they saw column after column of Union troops move in across the river. Soon Union General George McClellan had 87,000 men assembled across from Robert E. Lee's small army. Stonewall Jackson was very welcome when he arrived with reinforcements for Lee and his men. Still, the Southerners were vastly outnumbered. Lee sent cavalryman Jeb Stuart with a message to Ambrose Powell Hill to march as quickly as possibly to join them in the approaching battle.

About 30,000 Rebel soldiers were positioned in a line three miles long. To the north (the far left of the Rebel army) were woods, a cornfield, and a church. In the center, the Confederate troops crouched behind a sunken

lane. South of them, the men were posted in front of a bridge crossing Antietam Creek. Across the way, as night fell, a Union commander named Ambrose Burnside stayed awake planning a way to get his men across the bridge.

At the first light of dawn, Union artillery fired against the Rebel left flank. As soon as the smoke cleared, Union General Joseph Hooker sent his infantry charging across the field. The Union soldiers nearly reached the grounds of the church. Suddenly, they came up against John Bell Hood's Texas Rebel Brigade. The Texans were hopping mad. The attack had interrupted their breakfast—the first hot meal they'd had in days! Yelling like furies, they entered the fight at a run and the Union troops fell back stunned. A small group of the Yankees was stranded by the church as the Southerners drove the rest back across the cornfield.

More blue-coated soldiers swept in. For hours, the battle raged back and forth. First it seemed as if the North would overcome, then the Confederate troops gained ground. The Southerners were reinforced with the men from their center and right flank. The new troops struck the Yankees with all their fire. The soldiers' faces were black with powder as they fired, reloaded, and fired again. Thousands fell in minutes. The Rebel left flank held on by a thread.

A Slave Steals a Ship

Robert Smalls, a slave, worked at the Charleston harbor and was an excellent boatman. One night he fired up the boilers of a Confederate gunboat, the *Planter*, and headed out of Charleston harbor. Smalls dressed in the captain's clothes and imitated his walk on the deck to fool the Confederate guards who watched just inside the harbor at Fort Sumter. Union gunboats were blockading outside the harbor. Amazingly, Smalls managed to get out of the harbor unrecognized. He handed the ship over to the Union navy, saying "I thought that the *Planter* might be of some use to Uncle Abe." Captain Smalls piloted the *Planter* for the Union for the rest of the war.

At the center, D. H. Hill's men, behind the sunken road, faced wave after wave of Union soldiers. After holding the ground for four hours, the Rebels misunderstood a command and withdrew from their position. Union troops jumped in and with relentless fire gave the country road a new name—Bloody Lane. The Confederate center caved in. It seemed as if the battle was lost. But the Union troops were too confused and exhausted to continue the attack, and their generals did not reinforce them.

The battle was now most fierce on the Rebel right. For hours, three regiments from Georgia held 12,000 Union troops as they tried to cross Antietam Creek. Finally, the Georgians were reinforced, but even with help they couldn't hold the bridge any longer. Ambrose Burnside's Union troops crossed. The Confederates fell back.

Just as the Confederates were about to retreat, a column of troops approached from the south. The soldiers of Union General Ambrose Burnside's corps held their fire as the new troops advanced. They thought they were being reinforced but, to their dismay, the column was Confederate General Ambrose Powell Hill's division. The red-shirted Hill had marched his men double-time for 17 miles and arrived just in time. Hill's division struck Burnside's men hard on their left flank, and sent them falling back.

Finally, darkness fell. Lee's exhausted army held their ground the next day, expecting another attack. Always cautious, George McClellan held back. That night, the Confederate army withdrew across the Potomac River. The battle of Antietam had been the bloodiest one-day battle in American history. The South suffered about 10,000 casualties, the North about 12,500. Lee lost a quarter of his army. Hooker, describing the battle in the cornfield, said the cornstalks had been cut to the ground by gunfire as if they had been cut with a knife.

With the Rebels in retreat, Lincoln honored the victory by issuing the Emancipation Proclamation. Beginning January 1, 1863, slaves in the Confederate states would be made free. "In giving freedom to the slave," Lincoln stated, "we assure freedom to the free."

Blacks had been eager to enlist in the Union army, and after the Emancipation Proclamation they were allowed to do so. Northern blacks fought knowing that if they were taken prisoner they could be sold as slaves. Southern slaves made their way to Union lines to enlist and fight for freedom. White officers led the 166 black regiments that were formed. It was thought by some that the newly freed slaves wouldn't be disciplined enough in battle to lead themselves. The brave new black recruits quickly proved them wrong.

Acting Out Antietam

Gather some friends and reenact the battle to get a better understanding of events at Antietam.

What you need

A vacant lot, open field, or sandy beach—you'll need a lot of room to act out this battle

An army of kids (at least 10 Rebel soldiers and 20 Yankees)

Bandannas, strips of cloth, duct tape, or some other way to distinguish the soldiers on either side

Divide into two armies. For every Rebel, have two Yankees. Appoint your officers. General Robert E. Lee will command the Rebel army. Under him are Generals Stonewall Jackson, James "Old Pete" Longstreet, D. H. Hill, and Ambrose Powell Hill. General George McClellan will command the Yankees. Under him are Generals Joseph "Fighting Joe" Hooker, Edwin Sumner, and Ambrose Burnside. Finally, line the soldiers up in two rows facing each other. Several Rebels and Ambrose Powell Hill should stay off the battlefield for now. The battle begins!

1. Pretend that it's dawn of September 17, 1862. The battle begins at one end of the line when Union General Joseph Hooker sends his men slamming into the Confederates under Stonewall Jackson. Everyone at that end of the line should yell like furies and push back and forth. The Confederates are outnumbered, so send some reinforcements to that end of the line from the troops to their right. (Don't send all of them—some have to remain to hold the center!) This part of the battle took hours but you don't have to fight that long.

2. Next, Union soldiers are sent in toward the Confederate center. The Rebels there face their enemies from behind a sunken road and are relatively safe. Still, the Yankees keep coming. Send Rebel reinforcements from the troops on the right to help those men in the center. Suddenly, the Rebel soldiers receive word from a commander to withdraw from the sunken road. When they begin to withdraw, the Yankees jump in and nearly destroy them but don't have quite enough men to break through the line.

3. The battle moves down the line again when Burnside's men cross the bridge and attack. Since so many Rebel soldiers have been sent

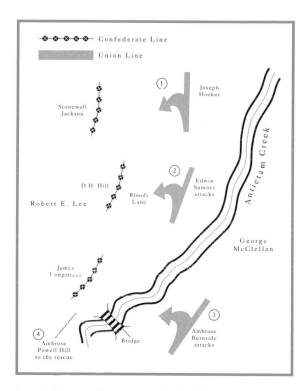

to reinforce other parts of the line, there are only a couple of men here to hold off many Yankees. The Rebel soldiers here should bravely hold the line. More Yankees should pour in and the Rebels should start to retreat. Now is the moment when Ambrose Powell Hill and his men come up. The Yankees hesitate— whose soldiers are these? Ambrose Powell Hill's soldiers crash into the Yankees and send them falling back.

Signaling with Wigwag

At Antietam and other battles, the artillery was helped by signalmen who climbed towers to see the enemy positions. They sent signals to the army to tell them where to shoot. The signals were sent by waving flags (or torches at night) in a system called "Wigwag." It was a dangerous job because signalmen were easier targets.

What you need

4 people

A flag or an old towel attached to a stick

Paper

Pencil

Have two friends send the signals and the other two receive them. The pair reading the message should write down the signal numbers and later decode them into letters.

Only 5 different signals will be used to represent the 26 letters of the alphabet. Use the chart on the next page to determine which signals you should use for each letter of your message.

Starting position (also used between letters): Hold the flagstaff with one hand at the bottom and the other in the middle. Hold the flag above your head in an upright position. Pause at the starting position for three seconds between letters.

Signal 1: From the starting position, wave the flag to your right, stopping at your waist, then bring it back up to the starting position.

Signal 2: From the starting position, wave the flag to your right, all the way to the ground, then return to the starting position.

Signal 3: From the starting position, wave the flag to your left, stopping at your waist, then bring it back up to the starting position.

Signal 4: From the starting position, wave the flag to your left, all the way to the ground, then return to the starting position.

Signal 5: From the starting position, lower the flag in front of you all the way to the ground, then return to the starting position.

A sample message, "Aim Right," would require these signals:

A	Signal 1
I	Signal 5 + Signal 4
M	Signal 5 twice + Signal 3
R	Signal 5 three times + Signal 3
I	Signal 5 + Signal 4
G	Signal 5 + Signal 2
H	Signal 5 + Signal 3
T	Signal 5 four times

Even this simplified version of Wigwag can be pretty complicated. It will help to write down your signals ahead of time and then make them slowly so that the team reading them can keep up.

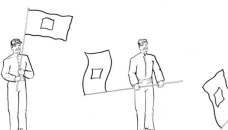

Starting Position   Signal 1   Signal 2   Signal 3   Signal 4   Signal 5

A	Signal 1
B	Signal 2
C	Signal 3
D	Signal 4
E	Signal 5
F	Signal 5 quickly followed by Signal 1
G	Signal 5 + Signal 2
H	Signal 5 + Signal 3
I	Signal 5 + Signal 4
J	Signal 5 twice
K	Signal 5 twice + Signal 1
L	Signal 5 twice + Signal 2
M	Signal 5 twice + Signal 3
N	Signal 5 twice + Signal 4
O	Signal 5 three times
P	Signal 5 three times + Signal 1
Q	Signal 5 three times + Signal 2
R	Signal 5 three times + Signal 3
S	Signal 5 three times + Signal 4
T	Signal 5 four times
U	Signal 5 four times + Signal 1
V	Signal 5 four times + Signal 2
W	Signal 5 four times + Signal 3
X	Signal 5 four times + Signal 4
Y	Signal 5 five times
Z	Signal 5 five times + Signal 1

Drummer boy Taylor

Black Soldiers

During the war nearly 180,000 black men served in the Union army and 10,000 in the Union navy. Thirty-seven thousand of them would die. Twenty-one black soldiers would receive the Congressional Medal of Honor.

In Deep Water

Half a day was wasted while Burnside tried to get his men across the bridge. No one seemed to know that there was a spot nearby where the river was shallow enough to wade. When it's muddy or dark, it's hard to tell the depth of water. Here's one way to measure the depth of a pond or river.

ADULT SUPERVISION IS RECOMMENDED

What you need

Ball of string

Ruler

A heavy rock

Pond, pool, or other body of water

Unravel a long piece from the ball of string and tie a knot in it every 12 inches. Tie the end of the string around the rock. From a safe place over the water, such as a dock, toss the rock in and lower it until it settles on the bottom. Pull the string back up. Measure the depth of the water by the length of the wet part of the string.

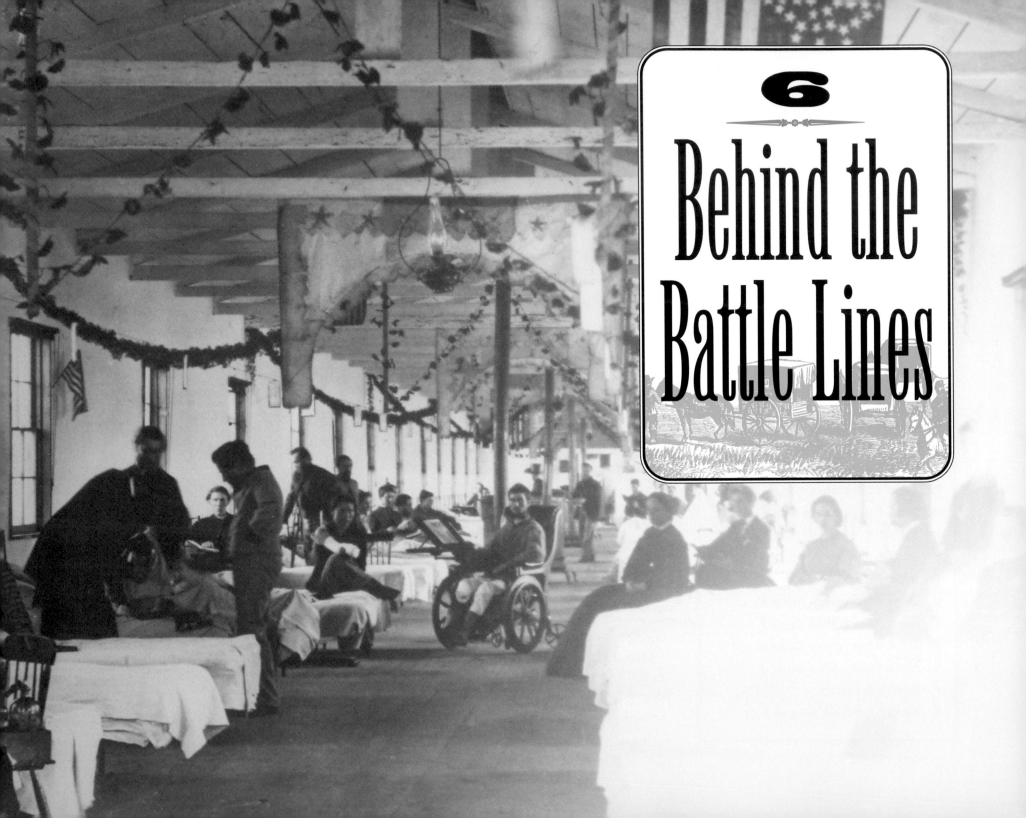

6

Behind the Battle Lines

As the battle raged at Antietam, a small, dark-haired woman appeared on the field with a wagon full of bandages, medicine, and blankets. The wounded soldiers thought they were seeing a vision. Clara Barton tended to the wounded without ever seeming to tire. One day, a bullet tore through her sleeve as she treated a soldier. He was instantly killed. Barton never mended the hole.

It would take more than a bullet to stop Clara Barton. The first woman to be hired by the federal government, she was a clerk in the U.S. Patent Office before the war. When she saw wounded men after a battle, she decided to devote herself to helping injured soldiers. She started her own relief organization. She raised money, purchased supplies, and took them by wagon to the battlefields. Eventually she quit her job to run the organization. The men called her "the Angel of the Battlefield." After the war, she devoted herself to finding missing soldiers, and located thousands. She lectured on her experiences on the battlefields as well as on women's rights. In 1881, this remarkable woman founded the American Red Cross.

Mary Edwards Walker

——◁▷●◁▷——

Walker was ahead of her time in many ways. She kept her own last name when she married, wore pants, and served as a surgeon during the Civil War. She was also a spy, and was imprisoned in a Southern jail for four months. She received a Congressional Medal of Honor for her service during the war. It was revoked because of a documentation problem, but was reinstated in 1977 by President Jimmy Carter.

In Richmond, Virginia, Sally Tompkins started a private hospital that had such success in treating soldiers that Jefferson Davis made her a captain. Dorothea Dix supervised thousands of female nurses for the Union for four years—with no pay. (Dix required her nurses to be over 30 and "plain.")

Women volunteered to serve as battlefield nurses. They brought the soldiers water and food, bathed their wounds, changed bandages, read to them, and wrote their letters. Mary Ann Bickerdyke traveled with the Union army for four years. She fed and cared for the wounded men and assisted the doctors during surgery. She was devoted to the soldiers and they to her. She called them her "good boys." They called her "Mother." Union General William Sherman, who didn't allow any women in his camp, bent the rules when Mother Bickerdyke insisted, saying "She ranks me."

On the home front, women raised money and collected supplies for the troops. Southern women donated family heirlooms and jewelry to finance the building of the C.S.S. *Charleston*, which became known as the "Ladies Gunboat." Church bells from towns throughout the South were melted down so the bronze could be used for weapons. Alert Clubs in the North sought out materials for the war effort and young boys called "Minute Men" hauled their wagons around town to collect the donations. The United States Sanitary Commission, created to provide soldiers with proper food and medical attention, received donations from people all

Clara Barton

over the North who raised money by holding fairs and auctions. President Lincoln donated his original draft of the Emancipation Proclamation for auction. The sale of this document and other treasures raised the then-astounding sum of $100,000.

Women took on men's work in addition to their own. They held jobs in weapons factories, where they made bullets and explosives. For the first time, many took positions as teachers, millworkers, and clerks. On farms and plantations, women and children worked very hard. They plowed, tended to the animals, cut firewood, and harvested crops.

Children took over the chores once done by their fathers and older brothers. Some worked in factories. But they also played and learned. In schoolhouses, they learned reading, writing, and ciphering (simple arithmetic). Many Southern schools closed down because communities could no longer afford to pay the teachers. In the winter, sledding and snowball fights were favorite activities. At home by the fire, kids whittled toys and made paper dolls. In the summer they swam, fished, and played baseball. They rolled metal barrel-hoops with long sticks. They had relay races and sack races and played games like Blind Man's Buff. Of course, a favorite activity was playing at war.

When their work at home was done, there was always something to be done for the war effort. Women and children rolled bandages and sewed blankets, flags, tents, and uniforms. Families sent care packages to their beloved soldiers. Wooden boxes were carefully packed with cured hams, woolen socks, writing paper, tea, and preserves. Every space in the box was filled. If they sent a pair of boots, they would tuck an apple or an onion inside. Always, they included affectionate letters sharing news

Abraham Lincoln and Jefferson Davis attended to all the business of running their countries in addition to conducting a war. A typical day for Lincoln began early in the morning, when he answered letters and signed documents. At ten o'clock, the White House was opened to all visitors. Many came to ask for favors, others just to shake his hand. When a particularly tall visitor came to call, Lincoln stood up to compare heights. At 6'4", he usually won. Meetings with his cabinet and high-ranking officers took hours. He visited army hospitals and camps. He reviewed soldiers' court-martial sentences and granted pardons to nearly all of them. Lincoln was so busy he often forgot to eat.

Confederate President Davis also had his hands full with paperwork and visitors. He, too, pardoned soldiers and revoked sentences. He visited his troops and, when a battle was fought close to the Confederate capital of Richmond, Virginia, he rode out to see the outcome. Davis was so anxious during the first battle at Manassas that he traveled by train and horseback to see firsthand what was going on. During the Seven Days' battles, Robert E. Lee had to scold Davis for riding into the line of fire and putting himself at risk.

Both presidents were cheered heartily by their troops when they visited camps. A graceful rider, Davis sat easily in the saddle. Lincoln looked a little less dignified on horseback. His long legs

dangled to the ground and the soldiers were tempted to laugh, wondering if he would trip his horse. With his great height and his tall stovepipe hat, anyone could recognize Lincoln from a distance. He became known for his famous hat, which he used as a safe, keeping notes and documents inside the lining.

Lincoln ran for a second term during the war. His reelection was not a sure thing. Many Northerners wished for peace, even if it meant letting the Southern states secede. Davis led the Confederacy for the length of the war, but it didn't always go smoothly. Many people disagreed with the way he ran the country and called for his impeachment. Some Southern states even wanted to secede from the Confederacy!

Lincoln's two younger sons liked life in Washington quite a lot. They turned the White House into one big playground. Willie and Tad, with uniforms and toy rifles, played at being soldiers all day long. They lined the servants up for drill. They built a fort on the roof of the White House with pretend cannons for firing at pretend Rebels. Tad rode a goat into the middle of a formal reception. Lincoln, who couldn't

say no to his boys, laughed when they invaded cabinet meetings. He wrote a pardon for Tad's doll, who was to be executed for sleeping at his post. His children begged him to also grant a reprieve to the Thanksgiving Day turkey (still a tradition of presidents today).

Oil on canvas, 22 x 36 in. Butler Institute of American Art, Youngstown, Ohio.

Snap the Whip

BY WINSLOW HOMER

from home. They sent useful items such as "housewives," which were pockets of cloth that held needles, thread, and thimbles. Since the men had to do their own mending, they were glad to receive them.

In the South, suffering from the trade blockade, goods were becoming scarce. Everything had to be made at home, from soap to candles to clothing. Old curtains and flour sacks provided material for clothes. Women made rope from moss and needles from thorns. Families suffered from food shortages just as the soldiers did. They learned to use blackberry leaves to make tea and dried yams or corn as coffee substitutes. Medicine was rarely available, so home remedies were made from plants gathered in the woods.

Sometimes the sacrifices required were too great. When the draft became law, a cry went up that this was a "rich man's war but a poor man's fight." In the North, if you had enough money, you could buy a substitute to serve in your place. In the South, anyone who owned more than 20 slaves was excused from service. In New York City, the draft started four days of rioting. A different kind of riot started in Richmond, Virginia, when a group of women, despairing at the scarcity and high cost of food, smashed windows and broke into the stores.

Because the war took place mainly in Southern lands, the people of the South suffered greatly. Sometimes battles were fought right outside a family's front door! Regiments would "commandeer," or take over, houses as bases for battle, leaving their dead and wounded on the

Union Forces Pursuing Confederates Through Mechanicsville

BY ALFRED WAUD

couches and carpets. Generals used fine mansions as headquarters.

In Southern towns that were occupied by enemy troops, the civilians were fearful. They had heard such dreadful stories of Yankee cruelty. Those stories were usually exaggerated, but the foraging soldiers did take most of their food, horses, and mules. When the armies of either side came through town, they ravaged the land. Thousands of men broke down fences and cut trees for their fires. The people who lived near the places where most of the battles were fought quit growing crops. Why bother, when their crops were always seized by the armies? Hams disappeared from drying-houses. Hogs, cows, and chickens were hauled away by foraging soldiers. Horses were taken for the cavalry. Sometimes the soldiers looted, taking the family silver and other precious objects. Even accommodating their own beloved Southern boys could be a burden, for everyone was hungry and had to be fed. After a battle, local women were called on to nurse the wounded. Houses, barns, schoolhouses, and churches were turned into hospitals. In these ways, civilians near battlefields experienced the war firsthand.

More difficult than the hard work, the shortages, and even the nearby battles was the waiting. Almost every family in the country had a family member or close friend in the war. After every battle, people frantically looked for news of their loved ones and desperately scanned the casualty lists in the newspapers. People waited for news, for telegrams, for letters, but mostly they waited for their husbands, sons, brothers, and friends to come home again.

A Housewife Sewing Kit

Soldiers filled these pouches with sewing supplies and used them to store small treasures.

What you need

A piece of fabric measuring 6 by 12 inches

A strip of fabric measuring ½ by 16 inches

Needle

Thread

Fold the top and bottom edges of the piece of fabric over ¼-inch and pin, then sew the hems. Fold the top and the bottom toward the middle so they each make a 2½-inch deep pocket. Fold the sides of the fabric over ¼-inch and pin, then sew the hems. Sew two seams, 1¾ inch from each side, on the bottom pocket. Turn over. Center the long strip of fabric over the housewife as shown. Attach it in the middle with a short stitch.

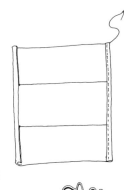

3

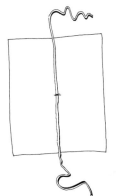

4

5

6

1

2

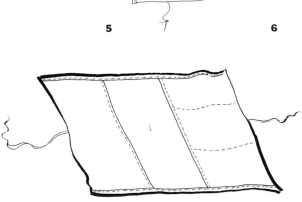

National Park Service

Civilians hiding in a cellar as shells fly overhead

WOODCUT FROM *HARPER'S WEEKLY*

Homemade Butternut Dye

Though the Confederate uniform was gray and Southern soldiers were called "graybacks," most of them wore clothes dyed tan (called "butternut") because this dye could be made cheaply from acorns or walnuts.

ADULT SUPERVISION IS RECOMMENDED

What you need

Nutcracker

36 walnuts in their shells

Plastic bag (you can use an old bread bag)

Cutting board

Hammer

Pot

8 cups water

Stove

Strainer

Large bowl

3 tablespoons vinegar

Wooden spoon

White T-shirt or other white shirt

Use the nutcracker to crack the walnuts and then remove the nutmeats (save for another use, or eat them as you work). Place the walnut shells in the plastic bag and knot the end. Working on top of the cutting board, use the hammer to crush the shells into small pieces. Remove the shells from the bag and place them in the pot with the water. Bring the mixture to a boil, then lower the heat and simmer for one hour. Turn off the heat and let cool on the stovetop for one hour. Pour the dye through the strainer into the bowl, then pour the liquid back into the pot. Heat it up again, then add the vinegar. Remove from the heat and, using a wooden spoon, stir the shirt into the dye. Let it soak for one hour. Rinse the shirt under cold water, wring it out, and hang it up to dry.

7

The Union Struggles

George McClellan, suffering from "the slows," didn't pursue Robert E. Lee to Virginia after the battle of Antietam. Lincoln finally had enough of his stubborn general and removed him from command. In his place he put Ambrose Burnside, a stout, balding man whose magnificent whiskers inspired the word "sideburns." Burnside had

twice turned down Lincoln's offer of the command. The West Point graduate had served courageously in the military but felt unqualified for the job. This time he accepted and, once in command, moved right into action. He would take his 100,000 troops over the Rappahannock River at Fredericksburg, Virginia. From there, they would march to the Confederate capital of Richmond.

Battle of Fredericksburg— December 13, 1862

When he learned of Burnside's movements, General Lee had the citizens of Fredericksburg leave town and placed his 73,000 soldiers there for battle. Stonewall Jackson held the Confederate right flank. James Longstreet's

What Did the Army Engineers Do?

In addition to building bridges, army engineers surveyed land to create maps, cleared roads, designed fortifications, repaired railroad tracks, and dug canals. It was said, "The Yankees can build bridges faster than the Rebels can burn them down."

Pontoon bridge

troops lined up along a ridge called Marye's Heights. In order to attack the soldiers on the Heights, the Yankees would have to cross a field under their artillery fire. Longstreet's artillery officer assured him that "a chicken could not live on that field when we open on it." Across the river, Union General Burnside worked on his battle plan. He would send his main force across the Rappahannock River on pontoon bridges. A smaller force would cross further downriver and attack the Southern right flank.

Special engineers called "pontoniers" hastily constructed pontoon bridges under the fire of

The Mud March
BY ALFRED WAUD

While the pontoniers worked, Union artillery lobbed shells across the river toward the waiting Confederates, setting fires and destroying homes throughout Fredericksburg. When the bridges were ready, the Union soldiers quickly crossed and the enemies skirmished in the streets.

Battle began in earnest the next day. The Union troops made a furious assault against the Confederate right. Stonewall Jackson's men waited until the Yankees were almost upon them before firing. The determined Union soldiers were able to drive a wedge between two Confederate brigades, but the Rebels soon closed the gap. General Lee, proud as he watched his men rally, said to Longstreet, "It is well that war is so terrible, or we should grow too fond of it."

On Marye's Heights, James Longstreet's artillery pointed down at the field below. Rebel infantry also waited at the base of the Heights, along a sunken lane behind a stone wall. Union soldiers crossed the field under relentless fire from both Rebel artillery and infantry. The Northerners made fourteen assaults, but not one soldier reached the sunken road. One officer said the men "melted like snow coming down on warm ground." Thirteen thousand Union soldiers fell in eight hours. The Southerners were astonished at the fearlessness of the advancing men. Later, Longstreet would write of the brave Union men who attacked his line, "I thought, as I saw them come again and again to their death, that they deserved success if courage and daring could entitle soldiers to victory."

Rebel sharpshooters. Pontoon bridges, made from large wooden boats, served well when there were no bridges to cross deep water. The pontoniers placed the boats in the water, side by side, until they spanned the river. They anchored the boats and tied them together. They laid planks across them, lashed them down, then covered them with straw and sand. Thousands of men, artillery carriages, horses, and wagons could cross on these makeshift bridges.

Union General Ambrose Burnside was in anguish over the terrible losses. He wanted to lead his troops in a dawn assault the next day but his officers discouraged any further strikes. He waited a few weeks, then moved the army upstream, planning to move around his enemy and attack the Rebels from the rear. As the Union army began its march, a torrential rain fell. Artillery carriages sank to their axles in the mud. Horses and men floundered. The army couldn't move! Watching Confederate pickets held up mocking signs saying "This way to Richmond." The "Mud March" marked the end of the Army of Potomac's fighting for that winter. They camped for the winter across the river from Fredericksburg. For weeks, the Union soldiers (who in spite of the battle and the cold, wet weather still had a sense of humor) said a new bedtime prayer: "Now I lay me down to sleep in mud that's many fathoms deep."

Meanwhile, the war raged on many other fronts. Union and Confederate forces struggled fiercely at Corinth, Mississippi. Armies moved across Tennessee and Kentucky and met in battle at Perryville. Forces clashed in Louisiana and Arkansas. In Missouri, the worst kind of guerrilla warfare raged. In another part of the western theater, Ulysses S. Grant was trying to reach Vicksburg, Mississippi. With Memphis and New Orleans in Union hands, only the Confederate stronghold of Vicksburg kept the Mississippi River from Union control. If Grant could conquer Vicksburg, the Confederacy would be cut in two.

General Grant sent Sherman downriver from Memphis with one force and took another himself by land, planning to close in on Vicksburg from two sides. General Grant's army hadn't gone far when raiding Rebel cavalry, led by Nathan Bedford Forrest and Earl Van Dorn, tore up its supply lines. The supply line (also called the "line of communications") was the route that the army used to bring in supplies and reinforcements and to send messages to commanders. Sometimes a road, sometimes a railroad, the supply line was of utmost importance. When the Rebel cavalry destroyed Grant's supply line, the Union army was forced to retreat.

The Confederate cavalry was a thorn in the side of the Union army. While Yankee cavalry recruits were still learning how to mount a horse, the Rebels were raiding. The Southerners' rural lifestyle made them much more accustomed to riding horseback. Confederate cavalrymen scouted enemy positions, and in battle were often the first to engage. They destroyed railroads and bridges. They captured prisoners and

The Battle of Stones River (Murfreesboro)

BY A. E. MATHEWS

supplies with surprise tactics that kept Union commanders up late at night, trying to figure out ways to stop them. This time, the Southern cavalry stopped Grant in his tracks.

Battle of Stones River (Murfreesboro)—December 31, 1862, through January 2, 1863

In Tennessee, two armies that had clashed for months faced each other again. The leader of the Union Army of the Cumberland was William Rosecrans, known to his men as "Old Rosy." The opposing Confederate Army of Tennessee was led by Braxton Bragg, a man men loved to hate. Bragg was bad-tempered and quarrelsome, but had the trust of Confederate President Jefferson Davis.

The Army of Tennessee was camped just north of Murfreesboro, straddling Stones River. Rosecrans and his Union Army of the Cumberland were camped so close to them that the soldiers could hear the enemy's regimental bands playing. One night in the Union camp, a band played "Yankee Doodle." Soon a Rebel band replied with a loud version of "Dixie." The two bands competed until one of them began playing "Home Sweet Home." The other joined in, and the men of both armies sang the words together. "No more from that cottage again will I roam / Be it ever so humble, there's no place like home."

[Lee] will take more desperate chances and take them quicker than any other general in this country, North or South.

—A SOUTHERN COLONEL, ON THE EVE OF CHANCELLORSVILLE

As the soldiers sang about the homes they had left behind, Rosecrans and Bragg drew up their battle plans. The commanders created nearly identical strategies, with each hoping to strike the enemy force on its right flank and center and push it back in an arc.

The Southerners struck first. The Union troops were nearly pushed into the Stones River. Union commander Philip Sheridan and his men, on the right flank, struggled to fend off the powerful Rebel attack. The fight was so intense that both sides began to run out of ammunition. Repeated assaults by the Rebels forced the Yankees back. The Confederates were only stopped when they reached a line of Union artillery guns, which held them off until blessed darkness came. Both armies were exhausted by the time night fell. After a brief push by the Rebels a couple of days later, the battle of Stones River ended inconclusively. Each side had lost one-third of its army. With Bragg's withdrawal, the Union claimed victory.

In the West, Union General Ulysses S. Grant tried every way he could think of to get to Vicksburg, Mississippi. He tried digging a canal across from the city to bypass the stronghold's batteries. He tried to send gunboats along creeks around Vicksburg, but overhanging trees knocked off their smokestacks and snakes and cougars fell onto the decks. Rebel infantrymen shot at them from riverbanks. It was a disaster! So many things went wrong that Abraham Lincoln's advisors suggested he remove Grant from command. Lincoln refused. He remembered Grant's victory at Shiloh. "I can't spare this man," Lincoln said. "He fights."

Lincoln did take Ambrose Burnside's command from him, describing his actions at Fredericksburg as "snatching defeat from the jaws of victory." He replaced him with the ambitious and confident Joseph Hooker. Hooker's nickname was "Fighting Joe," and he had lived up to it at Antietam and Fredericksburg. Lincoln asked him to destroy Robert E. Lee's army. "May God have mercy on General Lee," said Hooker. "For I will have none."

Hooker spent the winter months effectively rebuilding the Army of the Potomac and restoring its morale. When Lincoln visited, he was impressed with the troops. He was less impressed with their commander. Hooker said he had a grand plan. He seemed too boastful and sure that he could conquer Lee. Lincoln pointed out that "The hen is the wisest of all animal creation, because she never cackles until the egg is laid."

Gentlemen at War

President Abraham Lincoln brought his wife and son Tad along when he visited the army. Tad was thrilled when he saw real Rebel soldiers across the Rappahannock River. One enemy soldier from across the river recognized the tall president in his stovepipe hat. He took off his own hat and bowed.

Battle of Chancellorsville—May 1 through 6, 1863

Union General Joseph Hooker set his grand plan in motion. Leaving one-third of his army across the river from Robert E. Lee's forces in Fredericksburg, Virginia, he moved the rest around the enemy rear. After a long march and two river crossings, Joseph Hooker had 75,000 Union soldiers behind Lee's army and 45,000 in front of them. He hoped with these two forces to smash Lee's Army of Northern Virginia, which numbered only 60,000. Hooker made his headquarters at the crossroads of Chancellorsville, Virginia, 10 miles behind Lee, and sent his men east to attack. The soldiers moved through countryside so thickly covered with woods and undergrowth that it was called "the Wilderness."

National Park Service

An officer leading his men into battle
WOODCUT FROM *HARPER'S WEEKLY*

A Rebel Yell Contest

No one really knows how the Rebel Yell got started. Union soldiers later said that they made fun of it at first but soon learned that those howling Rebel soldiers meant business.

What you need

Loud friends

A tape recorder

Cornbread (optional)

Make up your own version of the fierce Rebel Yell. It's been described as "a falsetto yelp," as "a high, piercing scream," and a "series of yips constantly changing in volume and pitch." Some said it sounded like a loud "ki-yi!" Others said it was more like a "yeee-oooh!" When you hold your contest, first make sure no one nearby is trying to take a nap. Then gather your friends, turn on a tape recorder, and take turns howling like Rebels. Play the versions for a panel of judges. Give the winner an extra ration of cornbread as a prize.

Hooker's plan seemed to be working perfectly.

It might have worked perfectly against another general. Robert E. Lee, when he heard from his scouts that enemy forces had crossed the river in his rear, guessed Hooker's plan. Instead of slipping away from the impending crush of two forces, Lee made a bold plan of attack.

Lee ordered General Jubal Early to hold Fredericksburg with one division and sent 45,000 men to the west under Stonewall Jackson to meet Hooker. The column of Rebel soldiers met a division of Union troops on the road to Chancellorsville and a hot battle quickly developed. But just as the fight began, the Union troops received word from Hooker's headquarters. To the surprise of the men and their officers, Hooker ordered them to fall back. He said the thick forest wouldn't allow them enough room to fight. Some of his officers felt "Fighting Joe" Hooker had lost his "fight," but they obeyed his orders, moved back toward Chancellorsville, and settled behind defensive earthworks.

As the Union army dug in, General Lee rode to Stonewall Jackson's camp and met with him. They talked late into the night, trying to figure out a way to beat the entrenched Yankee force. Rebel cavalry leader Jeb Stuart brought them a

solution. He had discovered that the enemy's right flank was unprotected. This was interesting news, but in order to take advantage of it, Lee had to take a great risk.

Lee divided his army once more. He would keep only 14,000 men to face Hooker's 75,000, while sending Stonewall Jackson and his men on a march around the Union right flank to strike Hooker from behind! The gamble was enormous. If Hooker knew that only 14,000 men faced his troops, he would destroy them. Stonewall Jackson's troops, strung out on their march along a backcountry road, would be vulnerable to attack. The Rebels who were still left at Fredericksburg, Virginia, were outnumbered three to one.

In the morning, Stonewall Jackson's troops set out on the march, hiking for nine hours along little-used roads. They were spotted by Union "pickets" (army sentries), who sent word to Hooker that a Confederate force was on the move. Hooker was happy—he was convinced that the Rebel army was in retreat.

At six o'clock that evening the Union soldiers on the right flank were making coffee at their campfires when suddenly the forest around them came alive. Deer and rabbits bounded out of the woods into their campsite, followed by howling Confederate soldiers! Bugles rang and the Rebel yell resounded through the camp as the Southerners attacked full force. With fierce hand-to-hand fighting the Confederates pushed their foes back two miles before darkness brought the attack to a stop.

Stonewall Jackson wanted to continue the assault. He rode forward with his aides to survey the land for a night attack. As they rode back toward his camp, shots rang out. Mistaking Jackson and his party for Union cavalry, his own troops fired on them. Two of Jackson's aides were killed and he was shot three times.

Stonewall Jackson was down and Ambrose Powell Hill was wounded. Jeb Stuart took command of Jackson's men. The next morning he threw them against the Yankees while Lee attacked from another direction with the smaller force. The fighting was intense. Fires broke out in the woods and smoke blinded the men and horses. Union General Joseph Hooker ordered his men to pull in closer, and in doing so gave up a strategic location. Rebel artillery moved in and poured fire on the Union soldiers. Hooker's headquarters was hit by an artillery shell. He ordered his troops to another new defense line. At the end of the day, the two parts of the Confederate army met at the country crossroads of Chancellorsville. As Lee rode into the crossroads, he was cheered madly by his triumphant men.

Back in Fredericksburg, Union forces had captured Marye's Heights and now threatened to move on Lee from the east. Lee took yet another chance. He left Jeb Stuart to hold Hooker's army in its trenches and took a force toward Fredericksburg. After hard and fast fighting, the Confederates forced the invaders back over the river. Lee turned his attention back to Hooker. He planned an all-out assault for the next day, but when night fell, the whole Union army withdrew. Lee had won his greatest battle.

The battle cost the South 12,500 soldiers and one great general. Stonewall Jackson didn't survive his wound. Doctors amputated his wounded arm but pneumonia set in. Delirious, he called out to his troops, ordering them to prepare for battle. As he died, he cried out, "Let us cross over the river and rest under the shade of the trees." Lee felt the loss keenly. "I know not how to replace him," he said. There were 17,000 Union casualties. Abraham Lincoln was devastated by the defeat and loss of life. With the terrible losses here and at Fredericksburg, and Ulysses S. Grant struggling in Mississippi, it was hard to find reason to continue the war.

Some Famous Rebel Cavalry Leaders

Nathan Bedford Forrest, "the Wizard of the Saddle," enlisted as a private and ended the war as lieutenant general. He raised a battalion of hard-riding daredevils to terrorize the Union armies. His strategy was to "get there first with the most." Forrest was such a threat to the Union forces that William Sherman said he should be hunted down and killed "if it costs 10,000 lives and bankrupts the Federal treasury."

John Hunt Morgan disobeyed his commander's orders and led a raid across the Ohio River, throwing Northern citizens into panic. After riding 700 miles through Northern states, his raiders were captured and imprisoned. Morgan and his officers escaped and returned South. He was tracked down and killed by Union soldiers.

John Singleton Mosby was so successful in destroying Union outposts in northern Virginia that the region was called "Mosby's Confederacy." Once he surprised a Union general at midnight by capturing his guards, sneaking into his tent, and slapping him on the behind!

Jeb Stuart's famous ride around the Union army early in the war was the first of many escapades. Stuart served under General Robert E. Lee until May 1864, when he met his death at the Battle of Yellow Tavern.

Earl Van Dorn barely graduated from West Point, but fought fiercely in the Mexican War and on the frontier. Van Dorn was bold and reckless as a cavalry leader and in his private life. He was killed, not in battle, but in a fight over a woman.

Joseph Wheeler was chief of cavalry in the Confederacy's western states. This West Point graduate also led a ride around a Union army. After the war, he continued his cavalry career with the U.S. Army.

Rebel Cavalry at a Halt
BY ALFRED WAUD

Playing General

To win victories, commanding generals had to know the terrain of the battlefield and the strengths and weaknesses of their men, and had to make educated guesses about their enemy's next move. Acting out the Battle of Chancellorsville will show you just how challenging a general's job could be.

What you need

3 paper grocery bags

Scissors

Tape

Black marker

Blue and gray toy soldiers (or small sticks with ends colored blue and gray)

Cut the bags, lay them out flat, and tape them together so you have one large sheet of paper. Using the black marker, draw the map of Chancellorsville like the one to the right on the paper and use the map to reenact the Battle of Chancellorsville with your soldiers.

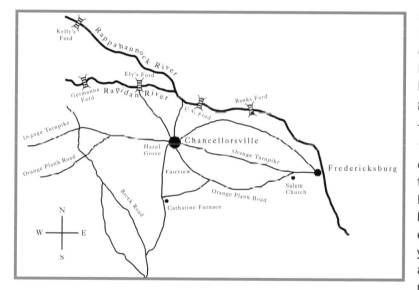

Before the battle started, The Confederate Army of Northern Virginia (60,000, commanded by Robert E. Lee) was camped on the west bank of the Rappahannock River at Fredericksburg. The Union Army of the Potomac (120,000, commanded by Joseph Hooker) was camped on the east bank. Each of your toy soldiers represents thousands of men who fought

at Chancellorsville. The starting point: Place your soldiers facing each other across the Rappahannock at Fredericksburg, the blue on the east bank and the gray on the west.

The Union army moves: You are "Fighting Joe" Hooker, and you order 18 blue soldiers to hold their ground across from Fredericksburg. Command 30 blue soldiers to move (very quietly!) west along the river. When you reach U.S. Ford, call "Halt!" and order nine men to cross the river. "Forward march!" for the other 21 soldiers to move on to Kelly's Ford. From here, command the soldiers to cross the Rappahannock and march to the Rapidan River—"Double-quick!" Fourteen men build a bridge at Germanna Ford and cross the Rapidan and seven march to Ely's Ford, swim the Rapidan, and spend a night in soaking-wet clothes. Allow your soldiers a short rest, then

order them to meet and march to your headquarters at Chancellorsville.

Lee responds: You are the gallant General Robert E. Lee, and nothing escapes your eye. You guess that the Union army is moving in from behind. Order six soldiers to hold Fredericksburg and send 18 toward Chancellorsville, marching along the Orange Turnpike.

The battle begins: General Hooker orders his men to march east toward the enemy. When the armies meet on the Orange Turnpike, the battle begins. After having second thoughts, order your men to "Withdraw from Chancellorsville." Arrange the soldiers along a line from U.S. Ford to a little south of Chancellorsville, then back north and west along the Orange Turnpike. Send a message to your men back at Fredericksburg to attack the city.

A daring plan: General Lee, seek out your "right-hand" man, General Stonewall Jackson, and devise a plan. Your scouts have informed you that the enemy's right flank is "in the air" (unprotected). You decide to split up your army

for the attack. Send Jackson with 12 soldiers on a secret march from the Plank Road to Catharine Furnace, to Brock Road, then along a lane west of Brock Road to the Federal right flank. Some of these men are attacked by Yankees at Catharine Furnace. The rest move on and reach their goal in secret. While they march, you distract Hooker by attacking his troops with only six soldiers. Stonewall's 12 soldiers attack the Union soldiers on the far right flank (give a big Rebel Yell here!). The blue soldiers retreat in panic and confusion toward Chancellorsville. General Lee's plan is a complete success, except for a great loss— Stonewall Jackson is accidentally shot by his own men. When the battle ends for that day, Hooker's line holds around Chancellorsville, Fairview, and Hazel Grove, with Lee's men around them in an arc.

Hooray for General Lee!: General Lee, order the six men directly under you and the 12 to the west to crush Hooker's army in a vise. General Hooker, command your soldiers to pull back from Hazel

Grove. Quick! Double-quick! Crash, bang—your headquarters is hit! Lee's troops move in and meet at Chancellorsville! Hooker, send an order to your Union troops to move to new defense lines close to the river.

A threat from the east: In the meantime, Hooker's orders to attack Fredericksburg have been carried out by the soldiers left there. General Hooker, move the Union troops to the west to attack Lee before he knows they are coming. General Lee, your scouts are always on the alert—you've heard of the danger to the east. Lead your men that way to attack.

The battle ends: General Lee, send your men to battle the troops from Fredericksburg. The Union soldiers retreat and they cross the Rappahannock at Banks Ford to escape. Bring the Rebel soldiers back to Chancellorsville for an assault against the rest of the Union army. General Hooker, order a withdrawal—bring your troops back over the Rappahannock River at U.S. Ford. You've lost the battle!

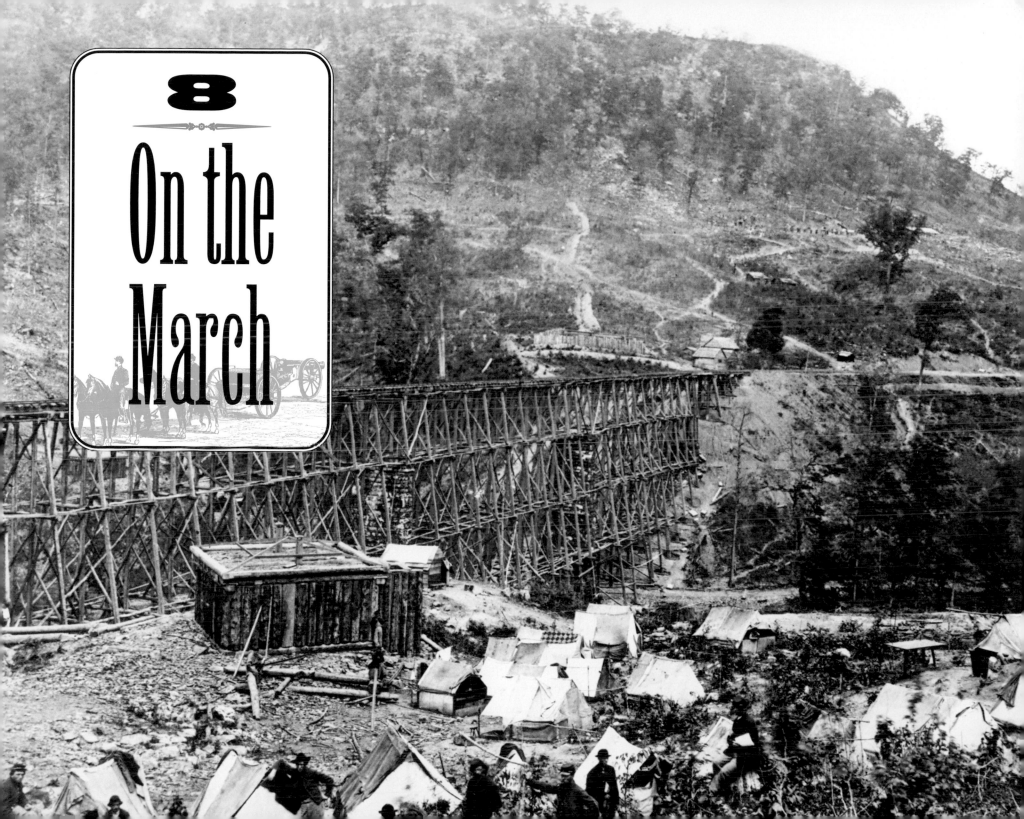

8

On the March

On the march to Chancellorsville, the soldiers of the Union Army of the Potomac each carried nearly 60 pounds of clothing, rations, weapons, and ammunition. For two days, they marched in the rain. After crossing the Rappahannock River on pontoon bridges, they waded the Rapidan. The water was chest-high, and that night they went to sleep muddy, dripping wet, and cold. Up at dawn on the third day of the march, they faced the daunting Wilderness, with its tangled undergrowth of brambles and vines. With each step, their packs felt heavier. With each step they walked closer to battle.

Even with the hardships, sometimes life on the march was better than camp. Marching meant something was happening. In camp, the days were long, especially in winter. Months of rumor about the war's progress came to a blessed end when the soldiers received a few days' worth of marching rations. Then they knew the time had come to pack up and go. They seldom knew where the march would lead them, but it felt good to go anywhere.

The night before a march they pared down their belongings. With all the weight a soldier carried, every ounce mattered. If there was time, they were allowed to pack personal items in a

Who Rode Whom?

———————

Robert E. Lee's horse was Traveller.

William Tecumseh Sherman rode Sam.

George McClellan rode Dan Webster.

Ulysses S. Grant loved all horses,
especially Cincinnati.

Stonewall Jackson went to battle
on Old Sorrel.

Jeb Stuart's famous rides were
on a horse named Virginia.

Philip Sheridan's horse Rienzi is
displayed at the Smithsonian
Institution in Washington, D.C.

box and ship them home. If not, anything they couldn't carry was burned or abandoned. The soldiers slowly reread letters, then burned them in the campfires, maybe keeping one special letter in a shirt pocket close their hearts. In the morning when the bugle sounded, tents were struck in moments. The men doused their campfires, shouldered their belongings, joined their regiments, and fell into line. At the signal to move forward, the march began.

Soon, long lines of men were strung out along the country roads. Flankers walked on either side of the marching column to keep a lookout for enemy troops. The supply trains followed—hundreds of mule-drawn wagons carrying ammunition, medical equipment, fodder for the animals, and food for the troops. There were wagons carrying pontoon boats and hospital wagons carrying the sick. Ambulance wagons also followed, a grim reminder to the men of what lay

Union column along the Rappahannock River

Famous Mascots

Old Abe, Robert Lee, and Stonewall were Civil War heroes of the animal world. These mascots traveled with their regiments. Old Abe, an eagle, was carried on a special perch by Wisconsin soldiers. Three of his bearers were shot from under him, but he survived the war and returned to Wisconsin. Robert Lee, who wasn't quite as brave as his namesake, was a dog who belonged to an artillery regiment. When battle broke out, he hid in an ammunition box. Stonewall was also an artillery dog. He showed up for roll call on his hind legs with a pipe in his mouth. A little dog named Jack looked for wounded men from his Pennsylvania regiment after a battle. Jack was captured by the Southern army, then exchanged for a Confederate prisoner. Cats, roosters, and tame raccoons also served as mascots.

ahead. The wheels of these wagons wore ruts in the dirt roads. The men were ordered to keep in formation, but often they dropped out to fill a canteen at a stream or well. At noon, they stopped for a meal.

Hooker loaded his men down with eight days' worth of rations on their march to Chancellorsville, but more often three days' worth were carried. These were packed in mens' "haversacks," cloth bags hung over the shoulder from a strap. A wallet, a bone toothbrush, tobacco and a pipe, a knife, and an extra supply of hardtack were among the items a soldier might keep handy in his haversack. The soldiers also shouldered their knapsacks and carried tin canteens, mess gear, and cartridge boxes filled with ammunition. In the winter they might also have a pair of blankets and an overcoat. If they had tents, each soldier would carry half a tent. When they stopped for the night, each would pair up with another soldier to put two halves together. Of course, they all had weapons. A rifle-musket added another ten pounds to the load.

If the days were warm the roadsides were littered with blankets and overcoats that seemed to grow heavier with each step. Even tents were discarded, especially on a summer march. Of course, what seemed like a good idea on a warm afternoon might be regretted later that night! When it rained, wagons and animals got stuck on

the muddy roads and had to be pushed. The soldiers pulled rubber ponchos out of their knapsacks or put their small tents over their heads and slogged along through the mud.

When it was impossible to make any progress through the mud, a group was assigned to build timber highways called "corduroy roads." They cut down large trees, laid them along both sides of the road, and covered them crosswise with smaller logs. They covered these with underbrush so that the men's feet and the hooves of the horses and mules wouldn't go through the cracks of the logs. If a small stream crossed the army's path, the men took off their shoes and socks, put their equipment over their heads, and waded across. If it was a deep, wide river, the engineers were put to work to construct a bridge.

Armies traveled by railroad, too. The railroads transported food, livestock, clothing, and munitions. Empty cars leaving the battlefront carried wounded soldiers back to the cities. Railroads were so important that cavalry operations concentrated on wrecking tracks, and many battles were fought over important railroad junctions. Movement of troops by rail played an important role in battles at Chickamauga and Chattanooga. Twenty thousand soldiers, their artillery, and their horses were transferred from the Army of the Potomac to Chattanooga in

*Union engineers bridging the
Tennessee River*

eleven days. This was the farthest and fastest any army had ever moved.

For the most part, the men marched. They marched day and night, up hills and down valleys, around and across mountains. They swam rivers, clambered over rocks, wound through dark woods. They marched on roads and across empty countryside. They marched in rain, snow, sleet, and under the burning summer sun. Sometimes they hiked for days without rations. Sometimes they slept on frozen ground. Sometimes they marched barefoot. Sometimes they practically marched in their sleep.

When they reached their destination, the soldiers made camp. They scoured the nearby countryside for downed wood or fence posts. Soon thousands of men would circle hundreds of small campfires to cook their evening meals. In winter camp cooks prepared the meals, but on the march the soldiers cooked their own. The Union soldier's marching rations included meat, desiccated vegetables, coffee, and sugar. Confederate rations might include bacon, cornmeal, rice, and molasses. Sometimes there wasn't any food. When that happened, the soldiers foraged in the woods for nuts and berries. If they were near farmland, the farmers' fields and orchards were soon stripped.

If low on time or supplies, Yankee soldiers settled for a meal of hardtack and coffee. Hardtack was the name given to the flour and water biscuits rationed to the soldiers. They were often so stale and hard that the soldiers called them "teeth dullers" and "sheet-iron

Build a Lean-to Shelter

If a soldier didn't have a tent, he could still have shelter by building a simple lean-to.

What you need

2 branches, about 3 feet tall, each with a fork
   at one end
4 long straight branches, about 4 feet long
An old blanket

Place the two forked branches upright in the ground, four feet apart. Lay a branch across them at the top, resting it inside the forks. Place each of the remaining three branches at an angle all along one side with one end braced against the ground and the other leaning against the top pole. Spread a blanket over these branches to make a roof.

crackers." Sometimes they were moldy or infested with bugs (which didn't stop the hungry men from eating them!). They ate them plain, broken up in their coffee or soup, or crumbled in cold water and fried in pork fat. They called this last dish "skillygalee." Coffee was the soldiers' favorite drink, and they parceled out their ration of it with care. If they wanted cream for it, they bought it from the sutler or "borrowed" it from a nearby cow.

Rebel soldiers fried coarse cornmeal in bacon grease to make a meal they called "sloosh." They also made cornmeal biscuits. They didn't have the luxury of real coffee, but made a substitute out of ingredients such as dried apples, peanuts, potatoes, or chicory.

After the meal, the soldiers gathered for a final roll call. Picket duty was assigned to some. The rest of the men rolled up in their blankets and fell, exhausted, into deep sleep.

Going into Bivouac at Night
BY EDWIN FORBES

Homemade Hardtack

Eating these tasteless crackers is about as enjoyable as eating a rock—and just as hard! Try dipping them in milk or water to soften.

ADULT SUPERVISION IS RECOMMENDED

What you need

Oven

2 cups flour

Mixing bowl

½ cup water

Wooden spoon

Rolling pin

Knife

Skewer

Cookie sheet

Oven mitts

Preheat oven to 350°F. Place flour in the bowl. Add water and stir with a wooden spoon until ingredients are well mixed. Knead with your hands for 30 seconds. Roll out the dough to ¼-inch thickness and cut into 3-inch squares. With the skewer, make eight holes in each square. Place on a cookie sheet and bake for 20 to 25 minutes. Remove from oven using oven mitts and let cool. This recipe makes 18 crackers.

9

The Confederacy Falters

icksburg, Mississippi, was practically a fortress. Batteries along its high bluffs looked over the Mississippi River, making it impossible for Union ships and boats to pass or attack the city. To the north, a swampy wilderness protected the city. Ulysses S. Grant's efforts to reach Vicksburg from the east were stopped by Confederate cavalry. The citizens of Vicksburg felt quite safe.

Grant's army waited on the west side of the wide Mississippi River, across from Vicksburg. He wanted to take his men across the river, march behind the city, and storm it. His soldiers were ready to help him but he needed boats to get them across. Union boats couldn't come down the river past Vicksburg's big guns. Or could they? Rear Admiral David Porter agreed to try the impossible. On a moonless night, Porter brought his gunboats and army transports downriver. The boats floated silently on the river's current past Vicksburg. On the west bank, Grant, his officers, and his family (who had come to visit him from Illinois) watched the fleet advance. Just as all seemed safe, the sky became as bright as day and a barrage of cannonfire bombarded the boats. The Confederates had spotted them. The river was bright with reflected fire. Grant's younger son, Ulysses Junior, cried and was sent to bed. One of the boats sank. The rest made it safely past the fortress.

Mississippians don't know, and refuse to learn, how to surrender.

—COLONEL JAMES L. AUTREY, POST COMMANDER OF VICKSBURG IN 1862

Admiral Porter's Deception

One time Porter had his sailors disguise a coal barge to look like a gunboat, with fake log cannons and barrel smokestacks. The fake gunboat floated past the Vicksburg batteries. A Confederate boat coming upstream turned and fled from it. When the barge was grounded by a sandbar, the Rebels saw it was empty and caught on to the trick. As they drew closer they saw that the boat flew a skull and crossbones flag and carried a big sign, "Deluded people, cave in!"

Admiral Porter's fleet passing the Confederate batteries at Vicksburg

The next stage was to ferry the troops across the river. Grant had General William Tecumseh Sherman create a diversion north of Vicksburg, Mississippi, and ordered a cavalry raid inland to distract the Rebels even more. The foray was a huge success. The Union cavalry roared through Mississippi, leading thousands of Confederate troops away from Grant's movements. The Union army crossed the Mississippi River and landed south of Vicksburg. They were outnumbered, and if beaten in battle there was nowhere to retreat. Grant said, "I was now in the enemy's country, with a vast river and the stronghold of Vicksburg between me and my supplies." He took a big risk, being cut off from his supply lines, but the important thing to him was that he was on dry ground on the same side of the river as the enemy.

U.S. Naval Academy

84

A 12-Year-Old Boy Goes to War

———— ·◄►◄· ————

Ulysses S. Grant's 12-year-old son Fred, stowed away on one of the boats and traveled with his father's army. He soon found out about the soldier's life. Grant didn't allow himself luxuries if his troops had to do without. At night, he slept on the ground, using his saddle as a pillow. The troops foraged for food, and Fred ate no better than the rest of them.

In Jackson, Mississippi, 40 miles to the east, Confederate General Joseph Johnston, recovered from his wound, was assembling an army. When Grant heard of this threat, he decided to strike Johnston before approaching Vicksburg. The last thing he wanted was to be caught between two armies. If he acted quickly, he could destroy Joseph Johnston's army before it was prepared for attack.

Over the next weeks, Grant's army marched to Jackson, Mississippi, then back to the river. Along the way they fought and won five battles. They drove Joseph Johnston's men out of Jackson, and that night General Grant slept in a bed, the same one Johnston slept in the night before. Grant instructed Sherman to destroy the town's railroads and factories. At Port Gibson, Raymond, Jackson, Champion Hill, and Big Black River, they beat Rebel forces. At Big Black River, Grant's 12-year-old son, Fred, was nicked in the leg with a bullet ("I am killed!" he cried.). Then Grant turned his attention to Vicksburg. Twice, the Union troops threw themselves against the stronghold, with no success and with great losses. Grant circled his men around the city and settled in for a siege. There were so many Union soldiers, a Rebel soldier said, that "a cat could not have crept out of Vicksburg without being discovered."

Eventually, Grant had 70,000 men entrenched in miles of earthworks around the city. They dug rectangular earthworks called "redoubts," triangular earthworks, or "redans," and earthworks in the shape of a half-moon ("lunettes"). Trenches topped with sandbags, called "parapets," protected the soldiers from enemy fire. The soldiers dug "saps," which were zigzag trenches, closer to Vicksburg every day. The Yankees dug one sap right to the edge of a Confederate fort. The enemy soldiers were so close they could talk to each other. The Yankees threw hardtack over the wall, and the Rebels returned the favor by tossing tobacco to the other side.

Inside, the 29,000 Confederate soldiers and 3,000 civilians waited for help. They hoped that Joseph Johnston would rescue them but Johnston never came. He was outnumbered by Ulysses S. Grant's forces and didn't think it was worth risking his men to save Vicksburg. The defenders of Vicksburg did their best without his help. Confederate sharpshooters picked off any Yankees who poked their heads above the trenches. Their artillery sent fire and shot into the ditches.

Day and night, Union guns fired into the city from land and water. The people of Vicksburg dug caves in hills. Called "bomb-proofs," the caves were reinforced with log walls and roofs. When it rained shells, the citizens of Vicksburg ran for their underground dwellings. People moved beds, chairs, and carpets into the caves to make them more comfortable and waited there, hoping the summer heat or Joseph Johnston would drive the Union army away.

Northerners had reason to fear, too. In the east, General Lee's army was coming their way. Lee once again took his army to the North. He hoped this invasion would lure Grant away from

Vicksburg, or, better yet, that a Confederate victory on Northern soil would lead to the Union's surrender. From their balloons, Union spies saw Lee's army move. Fighting Joe Hooker wondered if he'd be fighting Lee again.

Rebel cavalry leader Jeb Stuart was assigned to scout enemy movements and keep General Lee informed. Stuart was camped at Brandy Station, preparing his 10,000 cavalrymen for their mission. Early one morning, 9,000 Union riders charged his camp. The surprised Confederates jumped on their horses. The men grappled in combat, shooting at close range with their pistols while the horses reared and screamed. When their guns failed them, they drew swords. The contest was bloody and savage. Stuart's men held their ground but he was shaken by the surprise attack. Stuart had always prided himself on getting the best of his enemy.

The presence of 76,000 Rebel soldiers marching across their state terrified the people of Maryland and then Pennsylvania. Lee hoped to be well into enemy territory by the time the Northern army caught up with him. If Joseph Hooker had his way, he wouldn't have followed Lee's army at all. He wanted to attack Richmond, Virginia, instead. When Lincoln heard this plan, he telegraphed his commander with instructions to follow Lee's army. Lincoln soon lost confidence in Hooker, though, and as the Rebels moved into the North, Lincoln replaced Hooker with George Gordon Meade.

The appointment was a surprise, for Meade was outranked by others in the army, but he had served the Union bravely at Fredericksburg and other battles. A former engineer, Meade faced a great challenge. Within days of receiving the command, he would have to face that unbeatable Southern foe, Robert E. Lee. It made the tough and serious General Meade more testy than usual. The soldiers called Meade "an old snapping turtle," but they were eager to follow him to defend their land. The Union Army of the Potomac set off for Pennsylvania.

Jeb Stuart's pride had been hurt by the surprise attack at Brandy Station. He wanted to regain glory when Lee ordered him on this scouting mission. He led his cavalry on a raid through Northern towns. Because Lee received no word from Stuart, he thought the Union army was still far behind him. As he moved north, General Lee became upset by Stuart's absence. He didn't know the whereabouts of his cavalry scouts or his opponent. George Meade, however, knew the Confederates' locations. Lee's three corps, under James Longstreet, Ambrose Powell Hill, and Richard S. Ewell, were spread out near the towns of Harrisburg and Chambersburg, Pennsylvania. When a spy finally warned Lee that the Union army was north of the Potomac River, General Lee sent word to his commanders to gather their troops at a central point, the town of Gettysburg.

Battle of Gettysburg—July 1 through 3, 1863

The biggest battle of the war began before anyone was ready for it. An advance division of Ambrose Powell Hill's corps was sent ahead to scout the vicinity of Gettysburg. Their scouting mission became a hot battle when the division ran into Union cavalry under John Buford.

Gettysburg was a prosperous town of 2,400 people surrounded by farmland, orchards, and woods. Its citizens ran for shelter as a battle began in their quiet town. Mothers bolted doors behind their children. One woman stood outside her gate, slicing bread and passing it to the soldiers as they marched by, double-quick. An old man, John Burns, shouldered his rifle and joined the Union troops to fight. The Rebels had milked his cows and he was mad! Fighting beside the young soldiers, he was wounded three times.

John Buford's men fought desperately, outnumbered two to one, while both sides sent for reinforcements. Buford was an experienced soldier who knew the importance of good ground. When he scouted the area he noted two hills, Culp's Hill and Cemetery Hill, just south of town. From Cemetery Hill, a ridge ran a half-mile to the south. A position on these heights could make all the difference in a battle. If Buford and his men could hold the Rebels off until reinforcements came to claim that ground, all would be well.

The Union cavalry struggled to hold Hill's men back. Richard Ewell's corps arrived and joined the fray. The Confederates advanced, firing furiously into the Union line. Union general John Fulton Reynolds arrived with infantry to support the weary cavalrymen. As he placed his men for battle, he was immediately struck by a bullet and fell from his horse. His men fought on. The armies were engaged in full-fledged battle before either of the commanding generals arrived.

General Meade was 12 miles away as his men fought to hold their ground. He sent Winfield Scott Hancock ahead while he prepared to move to Gettysburg. By this time General Robert E. Lee had arrived and saw his men engaged in battle. He hadn't planned to fight at Gettysburg, but when he saw what was happening he threw all of his available men into the fight. The Union troops broke and ran through the town. Yelling Rebels chased them down the streets.

The day wasn't over. The Yankees rallied as they reached the hills south of town. Union General Winfield Scott Hancock arranged his men along the heights. It was a strong position. At the Battle of Fredericksburg, the Confederates' position on the high ground led to terrible losses for the Union. Now the Union army had the advantage. General Lee instructed Richard Ewell to take the hills, "if at all practicable." Ewell thought it wasn't at all practicable after the long and desperate day. More than one soldier described the fighting that day as the fiercest they had ever experienced.

The Union army lined up in the shape of an upside-down fishhook on high ground. At the end of the hook was Culp's Hill; to its west was Cemetery Hill. South of Cemetery Hill ran Cemetery Ridge, which ended at two hills known as Little Round Top and Round Top.

That night the Rebels heard the Union soldiers as they dug in and fortified their positions. The Union chief of artillery called it "bold high ground" and was happy. Though the Union army held the strong ground, Lee refused to withdraw from Gettysburg. "The enemy is there," he said, "and I am going to attack him there." He planned to send part of his army, under James Longstreet, against the enemy's left flank at the end of Cemetery Ridge while Richard Ewell's men attacked Culp's and Cemetery Hills. Lee believed these assaults would send the Union army fleeing.

While Longstreet prepared his men for attack, the Union left flank shifted. Against orders, Major General Dan Sickles moved his corps a half-mile ahead of the rest of the Union line. It was a mistake. His new position exposed his men—and the Round Top hills—to danger.

Finally Longstreet's attack was under way. His men moved against the Round Tops and struggled with their enemies among the boulders at the base of the hills. Two Alabama regiments advanced on Round Top. From there, they could see that Little Round Top was empty. If they took that hill, the Rebels could destroy

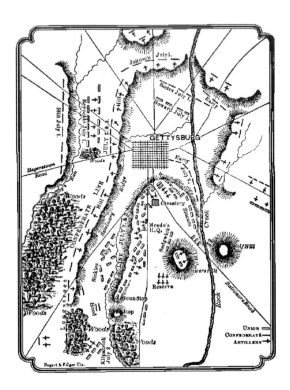

Map of the Battle of Gettysburg

the Union left flank—possibly the whole Union army. They moved in. Just in time, a Union brigadier general named Gouverneur K. Warren noticed that the critical hill was undefended. He sent for troops and a brigade moved to defend Little Round Top. They were told to hold it at all costs. Losing that hill could mean losing the battle. And losing the battle at Gettysburg could mean losing the war!

Colonel Joshua Lawrence Chamberlain, with the men of the 20th Maine, held the end of the line. A college professor, Chamberlain led his men valiantly, knowing that the whole Union army depended on the regiment's actions there. One-third of them were killed or wounded during the five assaults made by the men from Alabama. When they ran out of ammunition as the Southerners were gathering for another assault, Chamberlain ordered his men to "fix bayonets!" The Rebels ran up the hill. "Charge!" Chamberlain shouted, and the Maine men rushed toward the Confederate soldiers, who ran for their lives. Chamberlain would later receive the Congressional Medal of Honor for his brave command at Little Round Top.

Union general Sickles's men came under fierce attack, surrounded on three sides by the enemy. The air was thick with bullets. The nearby peach orchard and wheat field became scenes of carnage. Fierce contests gave names to the field that day—the Slaughter Pen, Devil's Den, the Valley of Death. In two hours, there were more than 4,000 casualties. Sickles's corps was smashed. He was wounded in the leg so badly

*The 29th Pennsylvania
Forming a Line of Battle
at Culp's Hill*

BY W. L. SHEPPARD

that his leg had to be amputated. (After the war, Sickles had his leg mounted and sent to a museum in Washington, where he would visit it!)

Other Confederate troops aimed for the part of Cemetery Ridge that had been left open by Sickles's move. As three Confederate brigades approached the gap, Winfield Hancock spotted a weak point. He ordered reinforcements there, but the Rebels were coming quickly. In minutes they would spill over the Union line. When the first regiment of reinforcements arrived,

Hancock asked the impossible of them. He sent the 262 men of the 1st Minnesota against the enemy in a bayonet charge. They stopped the assault long enough to hold the ground until reinforced, but only 47 of the Minnesota men emerged unharmed.

On the right flank, Richard Ewell's men had only a foothold on Culp's Hill. On this long day, the great efforts of the Southern army had gained little. The Union still held the heights. But Lee felt his men had come close to conquering the Union army, and that another day would bring victory. He planned to concentrate on the Union center, which he thought would be the weakest point. Jeb Stuart and his cavalry finally returned to General Lee's side that evening. He was ordered to threaten the Union right flank and rear if possible. A division under General George Pickett arrived too. These fresh troops would lead the next day's attack under James Longstreet's direction.

General Longstreet didn't want to send his men charging against the Union center. He thought the enemy position was too strong. Lee assured him that he would have 15,000 men, enough to carry the day. "General," Longstreet said, "I have been a soldier all my life, and it is my opinion that no 15,000 men ever arranged for battle can take that position."

At dawn, the Confederate brigade on Culp's Hill was struck by Union forces. Within hours, the hill was once again in Union hands. Richard Ewell would not be able to attack the right flank

George Pickett

———◆———

Wounded during the Seven Days' battles and long out of action, George Pickett felt honored to be part of this day's fight at Gettysburg. Slim and dapper, with curly brown hair that hung to his shoulders, Pickett graduated last in his class at West Point but fought bravely during the Mexican War and at Fredericksburg, Gettysburg, and many other battles of the Civil War.

Pickett's Charge
BY PAUL D. PHILIPPOTEAUX

again. The Rebel attack on the center would have to succeed on its own.

Longstreet ordered an artillery barrage against the Union center. He planned that the big guns would weaken the Union line, and then he would order an infantry charge under George Pickett. At one o'clock, hundreds of cannons exploded. Hurling shells filled the air. On the ridge, the Union army was caught by surprise.

Men were struck down while eating lunch. George Meade's headquarters was hit and he was nearly hit too. Union artillery responded, and for two full hours the armies fired at each other. The guns roared so loudly that they could be heard in Pittsburgh, 150 miles away. So much smoke filled the air that the gunners could no longer see where they were firing. In the hills, cannon shot tore limbs from trees, and rocks and dirt flew. The Union soldiers lay flat on their stomachs while shells screamed overhead. General Hancock slowly rode his horse up and down the line to give them courage. When an

The Gettysburg Address

Four months after the battle, Lincoln dedicated the cemetery at Gettysburg with a speech. In the Gettysburg Address, he praised "the brave men, living and dead, who struggled here." He reminded his listeners that the soldiers' sacrifices could best be honored by resolving that "this nation, under God, shall have a new birth of freedom—and that government of the people, by the people, for the people, shall not perish from the earth."

aide asked him to get down, he replied "There are times when a corps commander's life does not count." Behind the Confederate artillery, George Pickett's men waited.

Then, silence fell. The Rebel artillery, running out of ammunition, wanted to save enough to support their infantry charge. The Union guns, too, became quiet. Pickett, eager to do his part in this battle, looked anxiously for Longstreet to ask permission to advance.

General Longstreet, not wishing to send his friend and the men into this desperate charge, couldn't bring himself to speak. He nodded his head in answer to Pickett's request. Pickett rode back to his troops. "Up men and to your posts," he told his soldiers. "Don't forget today that you are from old Virginia!" With that, Pickett's Charge began. Though it now is called Pickett's Charge, other officers led brigades from Alabama, Mississippi, North Carolina, and Tennessee in this advance. Confederate and Union soldiers alike later said it was one of the most beautiful sights they'd ever seen. The column advancing across the field was nearly a mile wide. They marched forward steadily, their regimental flags waving. The smoke from the cannonfire cleared and the sun glinted on their bayonets. The Union troops waited quietly one mile away on Cemetery Ridge.

Suddenly, hundreds of guns went off at once. At times it seemed as if whole regiments were wiped out by the avalanche of shot. Flags fell and were retrieved; gaps appeared in the line and soldiers moved in to close them. They were fired on from the front and from the sides by two hundred Union guns. Every step brought them closer to danger. Soon they were exposed to the fire of Union infantry, and bullets poured into the line of men. Still, they kept on. They began to yell as they ran forward. With each step, men fell until thousands were strewn across the field.

Only a handful made it up the slope of Cemetery Ridge. At an angle in a stone wall where the Union line jogged forward, Confederate Brigadier General Lewis Armistead held his sword high and urged his men forward. He crossed the wall, followed by two hundred of his men. It was a short-lived triumph. They were soon under fire from their right, then brutal hand-to-hand fighting left them all dead or captured. Armistead was mortally wounded. His best friend, Union General Winfield Scott Hancock, lay wounded as well.

It was the end of the charge, and the end of the battle. Those soldiers who had survived fell back in retreat, struggling across the field under continued fire. Some walked backward so they wouldn't be killed by a shot in the back. The charge had lasted half an hour. Only a little more than half of the soldiers survived it. Just 30 percent of Pickett's division survived, and nearly all of his officers were killed or wounded. General Lee met the soldiers as they returned. "This has been all my fault," he told them. "It is I that have lost this fight." He asked them to rally and to help him as best they could. There was no need to rally at that moment, however. George Meade did not order a counterattack.

Friendship Between Enemies

Friendship between Yankee and Rebel soldiers was not uncommon. The pickets of the opposing armies were sometimes posted only yards apart. "Hello, Secesh!" "Hello, Yank!" they'd say, and agree to an informal truce. They shared daguerreotypes of wives and sweethearts, exchanged newspapers, and traded supplies. At Fredericksburg, Virginia, pickets made toy sailboats and sent them back and forth across the river loaded with items to exchange. At Petersburg, Virginia, the soldiers sent a dog between the lines with a can filled with coffee and tobacco hanging from his collar. One Rebel told of foraging with a Yankee picket guard. The two raided a farmhouse together and enjoyed a feast of honey, milk, and biscuits. The next morning the Confederate was warned by his raiding companion of an upcoming attack. "Go back, Johnny Reb!" the Yankee cried out, "We are ordered to fire on you." One young Rebel said later of his experience with a Yankee friend that "we talked the matter over and could have settled the war in 30 minutes had it been left to us."

The cavalry battle waged in the rear of the Union army was a Southern loss too. Jeb Stuart's attempts were thwarted by the Union cavalry, which included the "Boy General"—at 25 the North's youngest officer—George Armstrong Custer. The day was a disaster, and the worst day of General Lee's career. Longstreet would call it "one of the saddest days of my life." Of the 70,000 Southern men who fought at Gettysburg, there were more than 28,000 casualties. The Union army suffered 25,000 casualties in an army of 90,000 men.

The following day, the Fourth of July, Lee withdrew his troops. They carried as many wounded as possible, leaving the others behind to be tended to by the townspeople of Gettysburg. The Confederates marched back to Virginia. Meade told his officers, "We have done well enough." Upon reaching Virginia, Lee tried to resign his command, but President Davis wouldn't accept the resignation.

The people of Vicksburg didn't know about the events in the North. They only knew that their supplies were dwindling and food was scarce. People ate mules (and worse). They ran out of flour and made bread from ground peas. Even water was in short supply. As time went on, the shelling grew more nerve-wracking and the shortages more desperate.

Finally, the Rebel army could hold out no longer. They had nothing to eat. They had given up on the hope that they'd be saved by Joseph Johnston. General Grant received a message under a white flag, asking for terms of surrender. Grant agreed to release the Southerner prisoners if they gave their oath not to bear arms against the North. On the Fourth of July, Vicksburg surrendered. The long siege was over. Union soldiers entered the city and raised the Stars and Stripes over its courthouse. The Confederate troops stacked their arms.

The Yankees shared their rations with the starving Rebels. Grant said they acted as if they'd been fighting for the same side all along. A Confederate officer was told by a Union soldier that he'd tried to shoot the officer a hundred times. "Danged if you ain't the hardest feller to hit I ever saw!" the soldier said.

With Vicksburg's surrender, the Confederacy was cut in two. In the North, the news of the Confederate defeat at Gettysburg, followed by Vicksburg's surrender, brought huge relief and great joy. When Lincoln received word of Vicksburg's fall, he said, "Grant is my man and I am his for the rest of the war," and made Ulysses S. Grant a major general. The people of the South were shocked and saddened but they were not crushed. The war was not yet over.

10

Hardships of War

"It scares a man to death to get sick," said one soldier. He wasn't joking. For every Union soldier who died of a wound, four died from disease. There were a number of reasons for this sad fact. Crowded into camps with thousands of other men, the soldiers were exposed to contagious diseases that spread like wildfire. Many of the young men who joined the army had come from rural areas and had never been exposed to some of the childhood illnesses common in the cities. Suddenly thousands were down with the mumps and measles. More deadly diseases, such as smallpox, sent others to hospitals.

Unsanitary conditions in the camps, impure water, and bad diets added to health problems. Without fresh vegetables and fruit, many soldiers got a disease called "scurvy." Union soldiers in the South were exposed to malaria (which they called "ague" or "the shakes") for the first time. One million cases of malaria were reported in the Union army during the war. The men contracted typhoid fever and dysentery from bad water. Almost everyone suffered terribly from diarrhea. (The Union soldiers nicknamed this ailment the "Virginia Quickstep" or the "Tennessee Trots.") Sleeping in the cold and rain caused others to get pneumonia. There

What's in a Name?

—⊷◦⊷—

"Sawbones" was a common nickname for Civil War doctors.

were instances of men freezing to death in the winter. Confederate soldiers had few blankets or coats. There were times during the war when the men actually marched barefoot through snow and on icy roads.

Sometimes the cure was worse than the disease. The medications used in those times included strychnine and opium. Some of the medicines caused loss of teeth and hair and nerve damage. Many soldiers simply avoided treatment and tried to get better on their own,

Wounded soldiers being tended to in the field

but when wounded they had no choice. After a battle, stretcher-bearers went across the fields removing the wounded. Some were placed in crowded ambulance wagons and jolted along country roads to the closest hospital. The worst cases were tended to in the "field hospitals," tents put up near the battleground.

The minié ball was a solid bullet that, when it struck bone, shattered it beyond repair. Doctors couldn't do much to fix a man whose arm or leg had been struck. Amputation was often the only way to save a soldier's life. More than 40,000 amputations were performed during the War—three-fourths of the surgeries performed. The surgeons operated in the most primitive conditions, with the patient on a makeshift table of planks or a door torn from a nearby farmhouse. If the patient was lucky, some chloroform or ether was used as anesthetic. Sometimes whiskey was the only painkiller a soldier could get. Others were given a piece of wood to bite down on while the doctors quickly sawed off an arm or leg.

To make matters worse, doctors then didn't know what caused infections. They didn't clean their instruments between operations, and sometimes they held their knives between their teeth or wiped them off on their trousers. Wounds became infected and nobody knew that it was because the bandages were unclean or because they had used dirty water to wash the wound. Gangrene and blood poisoning were common.

The Red Badge of Courage

―――⇒⧫⧫⇐―――

To "show the white feather" meant to run away from battle. A wound received in battle was called a "red badge of courage."

One corporal refused to let the doctors take off his leg. When the surgeon came near, he drew a pistol, pointed it at the doctor, and said, "The man that puts a hand on me dies!" The surgeon shrugged and went on to the next patient. The man lived to tell the tale and his leg recovered from the wound.

When a battle occurred near a town, it was up to the local people to help the wounded. The people of Gettysburg had more than 20,000 wounded soldiers to tend to when the battle ended. Every house became a hospital and every spare person became a nurse. Even if they didn't know much about medicine, care and loving kindness did something toward helping the men heal.

The casualty rates during the Civil War were extremely high compared to wars before and since that time. This was because of a deadly combination of modern weapons and old-fashioned military tactics. Soldiers were ordered to attack in long columns and advance close to the enemy before firing. These tactics worked well in the days of the smoothbore musket, which didn't fire very accurately or very far. Back then, soldiers could get close to the enemy without getting shot. Right before the Civil War, the rifle-musket was invented. This weapon could kill at a greater distance. A column of advancing soldiers could be mowed down by enemy fire long before they themselves were ordered to

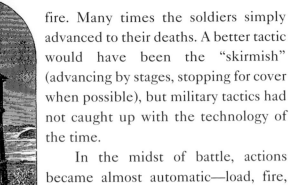

fire. Many times the soldiers simply advanced to their deaths. A better tactic would have been the "skirmish" (advancing by stages, stopping for cover when possible), but military tactics had not caught up with the technology of the time.

In the midst of battle, actions became almost automatic—load, fire, and reload. Some soldiers described a sort of battle frenzy that came over them and directed their actions. The moments before the battle were sometimes more terrifying than the actual event. Tension mounted until it was almost unbearable. Some soldiers prayed. Some made jokes to cover their nervousness. There were men who seemed to know that their death was near. Many wrote their names on scraps of paper and stuck them in their shirts so their bodies could be identified after death.

The beat of drums called the soldiers into formation. Regimental flags were lifted and unfurled in the wind. The flags, inscribed with the names of battles they'd survived, gave the soldiers hope they'd survive this one, too, and served as a rallying point for the men. "Fall in!" the commanders shouted. "Forward march!" Soon the deafening noise of battle began. Guns roared, officers shouted out orders, men ran forward yelling. Horses screamed, and the wounded cried out in pain. Guns became hot, almost too hot to touch. The soldiers' faces were blackened with gunpowder. The men became deaf and numb from the noise and exertion and some thought that the very air around them was red. Afterward, exhausted, maybe wounded or suffering the loss of a friend, they might have to quickly retreat to avoid capture.

More than 400,000 soldiers were taken prisoner during the course of the war. There were approximately 150 prisons throughout the North and South. Generally, officers and enlisted men were sent to different facilities. All were fearful places. When the war began, each side thought it wouldn't last long. No one gave thought to building proper prisons for holding enemy soldiers. As the war went on, local jails quickly filled up. Warehouses and schools were turned into makeshift prisons. When they became too crowded, prisoners were simply kept in open fields. In the South, where some areas suffered from food shortages and transportation problems, prisoners were the last to get food, clothing, or blankets. Union officials, angered by the

Three Confederate prisoners from the Battle of Gettysburg

Libby Prison

treatment their soldiers were receiving in the Southern prisons, cut back on rations to Confederate prisoners.

For a while the two governments agreed to exchange prisoners. In 1863, this system broke down, and the prisoners were left to suffer in overcrowded, makeshift prison camps until the war ended. Approximately 56,000 soldiers died in prison. Many others suffered from the experience for the rest of their lives. At the Union prison of Johnson's Island in Lake Erie, prisoners froze to death during the cold winters. From Camp Douglas in Chicago to Belle Isle near Richmond, the men waited anxiously for release.

At Elmira Prison in New York, prisoners were given little food and no medical care. One-fourth of them died from exposure during a bitterly cold winter. In the South, Camp Sumter (better known as Andersonville) held nearly 45,000 Union soldiers during the 14 months of its existence. Over 13,000 died; those who survived were nearly skeletons. The prisoners lived crowded together in a 26-acre open pen. In the summer, the fierce hot Georgia sun beat down on them. In the winter they suffered through the cold rains. Their rations were next to nothing. The creek that ran through the camp and served as their water supply was soon contaminated. Without clean water no one could survive. One night during a fierce storm, a spring erupted where no water had flowed before. The men felt the fresh water was a gift from above, and named it Providence Spring.

ACTIVITY

A Makeshift Stretcher

What you need

An old blanket

Two sturdy broomsticks

Lay the blanket flat on the ground. Put one of the broomsticks on the blanket about one-third of the way from one side. Fold the third of the blanket over the broomstick (as shown). Place the other broomstick six inches from the edge of the side you just folded over. Fold the six inches back over this broomstick. Next, fold the rest of the blanket over the top. Carefully lift your wounded soldier onto the stretcher.

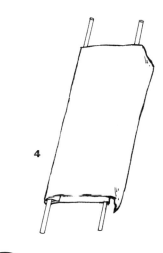

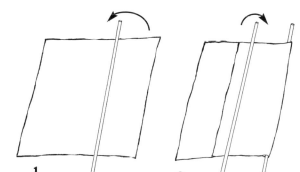

1   2   3

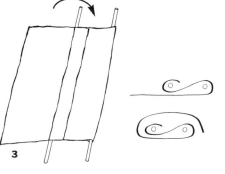

Libby Prison, a converted tobacco warehouse in Richmond, Virginia, housed Union officers. Using knives, a bucket, and one old chisel, a group of prisoners dug a tunnel under a wall and beneath the prison yard. When they thought they'd dug far enough, one of the men wiggled through and stuck his head out—only to find himself still several feet away from the outer wall. Confederate guards stood talking right next to him! He quickly pulled his head back in and plugged the hole. The prisoners continued to dig. Finally, the tunnel was completed and 109 men made their escape. Half were recaptured; the rest disappeared in the streets of Richmond. Some found help in the homes of Union sympathizers, and others made their way along country roads, back to the Union lines.

99

Battlefield Bandages

Warning—The following activities are to be used on pretend-wounded comrades in battle reenactments. Don't try to treat a real wounded person unless you've had training in first aid.

What you need

A square of cloth measuring 36 by 36 inches

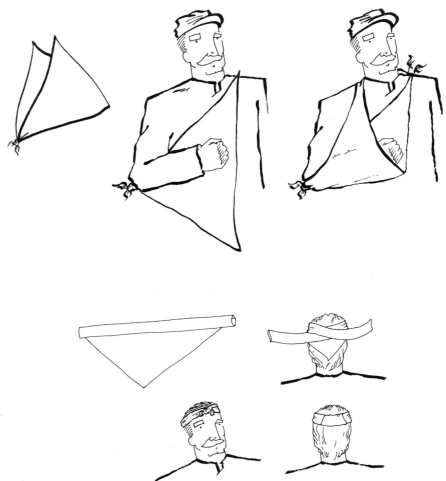

1. Fold the cloth into a triangle. Tie a knot in one corner of it so that it makes a little pocket. Place the cloth over the wounded person's chest (as shown) with the knotted end under the person's right elbow, so that the elbow rests in the pocket. Drape one corner of the cloth over the person's left shoulder. Bring the other corner over the injured right arm, over the right shoulder, and around the neck. Tie the two ends together behind the neck. (These instructions are for a right arm wound; reverse them for a wounded left arm.)

2. You can use the cloth to wrap a head wound, too. Fold it into a triangle. Fold one edge over twice (as shown). Wrap the cloth around the patient's head, with the point hanging down the nape of the neck. Cross the other ends around the back of the head and tie them together at the forehead. Tuck the triangular point over the cloth in the back.

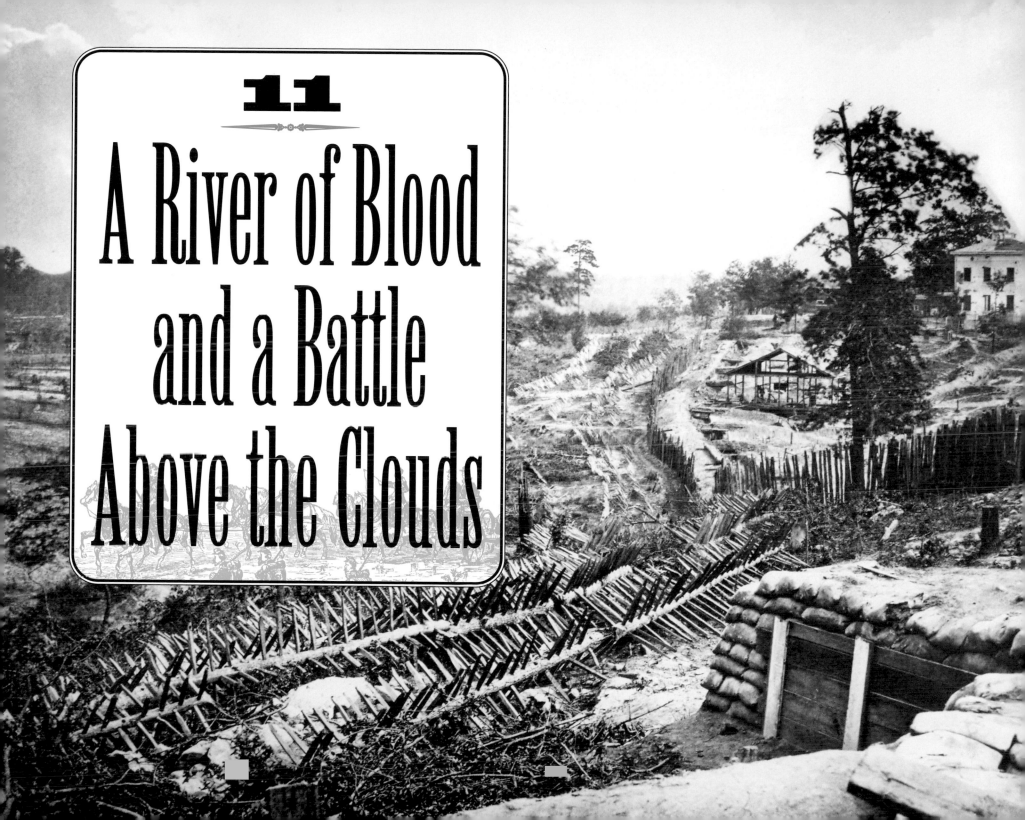

11

A River of Blood and a Battle Above the Clouds

In the east, Robert E. Lee had retreated from Gettysburg, Pennsylvania. In the west, Ulysses S. Grant had conquered the Confederate stronghold of Vicksburg, Mississippi. But in Tennessee, two armies had been confronting each other for months with no outcome. While Braxton Bragg held Chattanooga, Tennessee, with his Confederate Army of Tennessee, Union General William Rosecrans prepared to move against him with the Army of the Cumberland.

After months of preparation, Rosecrans swung into action. He was too late to trap his enemy in Chattanooga. Bragg's spies had informed him that columns of Yankee soldiers were on the march. Bragg slipped his army away from the city to meet the enemy on better ground. He sent for reinforcements, too. Three divisions under Confederate General James Longstreet rode the rails from Virginia to the wooded land just over the Georgia state line, around a creek called Chickamauga.

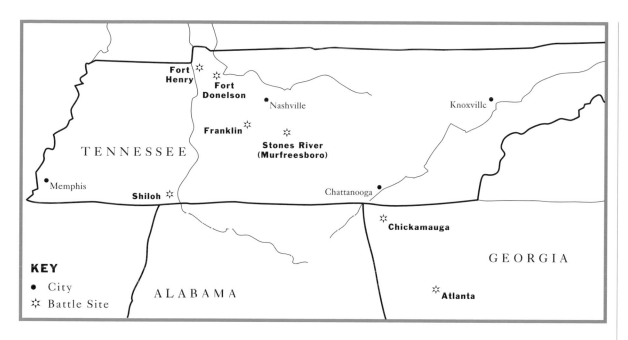

Map of Tennessee and Georgia showing some of the battles fought in these states

Battle of Chickamauga— September 19 through 20, 1863

Longstreet's men spilled out from the passenger cars, mail cars, and coal cars to reinforce the Confederate troops. That night, the Rebels forced a crossing of the Chickamauga Creek, in preparation for a strike against the Yankee forces in the morning.

Longstreet and his aides mounted their horses and rode through the dark forests late that night, looking for General Bragg's headquarters. Suddenly, they rode right into the Union lines! A Yankee sentry called out "Who goes there?" It was too dark to see their uniforms. Longstreet, thinking quickly, disguised his Southern accent and convinced the guard he was friend, not foe.

Finally, he reached Confederate headquarters and received his instructions for the following day. Tomorrow at dawn they would attack.

The Union army beat them to the punch with a furious attack against the Confederate right flank. The Rebels responded bravely. Each side was reinforced; each gave ground only to take it back again. Chickamauga Creek ran red with real blood that day as the armies attacked and counterattacked.

The men fought in a dense forest along a four-mile line, ducking behind trees to reload, then moving forward. The roar of murderous fire was described by one soldier as a "solid, unbroken wave of awe-inspiring sound." A Rebel division broke through the Union center, only to be thrown back by Yankee reinforcements. John Bell Hood led his howling Texans in a fierce attack that came close to taking Union General Rosecrans's headquarters. Again the Union line closed as reinforcements arrived. As the sky darkened, a Confederate division moved in and poured fire over shocked Union troops, who thought the fighting had ended for the day. The night was long and cold, and many of the men stayed up late, feverishly building "breastworks" (chest-high earthen fortifications) for the next day's fight.

The next day the men continued their fearful battle. Wave after wave of Confederate soldiers smashed into the Union fortifications. Union General George Thomas and his men, holding up against heavy Rebel fire, were desperate for reinforcements. General William

Scattered wounded on a battlefield
WOODCUT FROM *HARPER'S WEEKLY*

Rosecrans moved troops from different parts of the line to help the men under this fierce fire.

In the confusing fight in the woods, it was difficult for the generals to see what was going on. Rosecrans received a report that a gap had appeared at the center of his line. He ordered a division to fill the breach. The report was wrong, and now there was a real gap where that division used to be! Just at that moment, Longstreet sent his Rebel forces into the quarter-mile gap. With a great shout, his soldiers charged and swarmed over the Union line. Confused Yankees ran in panic. The Confederates overran Union head-quarters, and General Rosecrans escaped just in time. Thousands of Union soldiers raced to the rear. Rosecrans retreated to Chattanooga. All seemed lost.

Rosecrans believed his entire army had retreated, but one Union general, George Thomas, still held. He lined his men along a hill and held the ground against terrific odds, attacked by James Longstreet from one direc-tion and General Leonidas Polk from the other. Again and again, the Rebels clambered up the hill. The Union soldiers were nearly out of ammunition. How much longer could they hold

What's in a Name?

Chickamauga is a Cherokee name meaning "River of Blood."

George Thomas

Though he was from Virginia, George Thomas remained loyal to the Union after secession. This determined and brave fighter was a West Point graduate and a veteran of the Mexican War. Thomas's nickname was "Old Pap" until Chickamauga, when he received the nickname "the Rock of Chickamauga."

up against what seemed to be the whole Confederate army? As hope faded, Thomas saw a column of troops marching toward him. He was afraid it was a Rebel brigade and wondered how his men could hold up against any more. To his great relief the soldiers were dressed in blue. The reinforcements were welcomed by Thomas's exhausted men. Together they held the hill. James Longstreet later wrote that he sent 25 attacks against General Thomas at Chickamauga. Some of these attacks pierced the Union lines, but Thomas's men fought savagely and threw the Rebels back.

Late in the afternoon, Union General William Rosecrans's chief-of-staff, James Garfield, arrived at Thomas's side. Garfield, exhausted and his horse injured, explained to Thomas that his was the only part of the line that had held. He would get no support and must withdraw. With little ammunition left, Thomas led his men in an orderly withdrawal to join the rest of the army in Chattanooga. They had made a brave stand against great odds, and George Thomas would from then on be known as "the Rock of Chickamauga."

There were more than 34,000 casualties during the two-day battle. Though more were Confederate casualties, it was a major victory for the South. But Confederate General Braxton Bragg seemed reluctant to believe he'd won, even though the Union army was licking its wounds in Chattanooga. Bragg's officers were angry that he didn't follow and destroy the Union army. Bragg chose instead to occupy the hills around Chattanooga and try to starve the Northerners out.

William Rosecrans had also hoped to occupy Chattanooga, but not under these conditions. Rebel guns pointed down at the Union camps from the heights above the city—Missionary Ridge and Lookout Mountain. The Union army was under siege, and it wasn't long before the troops and the townspeople ran out of food.

Help was on the way in the form of a rumpled general from the west. By special order of President Lincoln, Ulysses S. Grant was given command of the western armies. He moved quickly on receiving the promotion. He sent orders to replace William Rosecrans with George Thomas, "the Rock of Chickamauga," and ordered Thomas to hold Chattanooga at all costs. Thomas replied that his men would hold "till we starve," which perhaps wouldn't be long. Two corps under Joseph Hooker were detached from the Union Army of the Potomac and sent west to Chattanooga on trains. Twenty thousand more Union troops under General William Tecumseh Sherman were ordered to Chattanooga from the west. Grant then organized a force to push the Rebels away from the Tennessee River and get food and supplies into the camps. The soldiers were even glad to see hardtack again.

Still, Confederate General Braxton Bragg felt confident. The Confederates held the high ground above the city and the Yankees would be hard pressed to escape from under their guns.

Presidents Who Served in the Civil War

——————◦❉◦——————

James Garfield would one day be president of the United States. Other U.S. presidents who served in the Civil War include Andrew Johnson, Ulysses S. Grant, Rutherford B. Hayes, Chester Arthur, Benjamin Harrison, and William McKinley.

Bragg even sent James Longstreet's divisions away. This reduced the number of Confederate troops surrounding Chattanooga. They would be missed.

Battle of Chattanooga (Lookout Mountain and Missionary Ridge)—November 23 through 25, 1863

As soon as all the reinforcements arrived, General Grant put all of the combined forces into action. Grant ordered William Tecumseh Sherman to attack the Rebel right flank at the end of Missionary Ridge. Joseph Hooker would launch an attack against Lookout Mountain on the left at the same time. If successful, his men would push from there toward the Rebel center. George Thomas, in the meantime, was instructed to "demonstrate," or pretend he was going to attack, at the center of the Rebel line. He would keep the enemy too worried to send reinforcements to the flanks.

Sherman's men made great efforts but gained little ground that day. Hooker was more successful. His soldiers advanced up the slopes of Lookout Mountain, which was blanketed in fog and mist. They attacked the first line of Confederates on the slopes and sent them flying. Artillery shells rained on them from above as they continued their climb. Two more assaults fought on the mountain's sheer face resulted in a Union victory. The desperate fight on the mountain was named "The Battle Above the Clouds."

It ended with a Union flag flying from the peak, and the Confederate troops falling back in retreat toward Missionary Ridge.

The next day, the fight resumed. Hooker fought from the left and Sherman's men once again attacked on the Confederate right. Time after time, Sherman sent his soldiers in but they made no progress against the staunch Confederate line. Watching the battle through his field glasses, General Grant saw that the only way to help Sherman was to attack the Confederate center.

The men ordered to make this attack on the center were the same troops who had retreated from Chickamauga. They quickly accomplished their assigned goal—to advance to the base of Missionary Ridge. Here, they were told to stop until further orders. Against commands, the men kept going! They'd been beaten by these Rebels and wanted revenge. "Remember Chickamauga!" they shouted as they ran up the ridge under a barrage of fire. They attacked the Southern troops with such violence that the Confederates were driven out of their fortifications. The Confederate Army of Tennessee retreated and Union flags flew along the length of Missionary Ridge.

Braxton Bragg sent his resignation to President Davis, who accepted it sadly. Joseph Johnston would now take command of the Confederate Army of Tennessee. President Lincoln declared an official day of thanks, the country's first national Thanksgiving. The people of the North celebrated the victorious battle of Chattanooga and prayed that the war would soon be over.

"**I** am lying out in the pine-woods ... ready to wield my pencil when the struggle begins," wrote Frank Vizetelly right before the battle of Fredericksburg. This British journalist wrote firsthand accounts of battles for nearly the entire length of the war. He traveled on Union navy gunboats to Memphis and rode with a Union cavalry regiment as they fought their way south. Then he switched sides, reporting the Confederate

viewpoint from Fredericksburg, Vicksburg, and the battle of Chickamauga. He sailed with a Confederate blockade-runner and attended society balls in Richmond, Virginia. Vizetelly's reports of his experiences in America gave his readers a clear idea of what was going on in that war-torn land. He was one of hundreds of reporters and artists who traveled with the armies to cover the War.

Some of the generals, especially William Tecumseh Sherman, hated having reporters around. Sherman felt they were no better than spies. Reporters gave away troop movements and numbers to anyone who could read a newspaper—including enemy generals. George Meade was so angry with one reporter that he sent him across battle lines to the Confederates.

Walt Whitman

Reporting was difficult and dangerous work. The reporters placed themselves near the battlefields as the armies clashed. Bullets whizzed past their heads as they tried to sketch and write. They struggled to see the movements of troops in the smoke and confusion of battle so they could describe their actions. They rushed their sketches and reports to the offices of such papers as *Harper's Weekly* and *Frank Leslie's Illustrated Newspapers*.

Two brothers, Alfred and William Waud, were sketch artists who made many illustrations at the battlefront. Winslow Homer, who later became a famous painter, sketched and painted Civil War scenes. He witnessed the naval battle of the *Monitor* and *Virginia* and was with the Union army at the end of the war. Thomas Nast and Edwin Forbes were two other famous artists of the Civil War era. They worked at battles from Antietam to Gettysburg.

The story of the war was told by others too. A British colonel, Arthur Freemantle, traveled with the Confederate armies and later published the journal he kept of his adventures. He was an eyewitness at Gettysburg:

> The firing along the whole line was as heavy as it is possible to conceive. A dense smoke arose and the air seemed full of shells. When the cannonade was at its height, a Confederate band began to play polkas and waltzes, which sounded very curious, accompanied by the hissing and bursting of the shells.

Soldiers told the war's story in letters and diaries. Some wrote books about their experiences.

Private Sam Watkins of the 1st Tennessee Infantry wrote *Co. Aytch*. Among other battles, he described fighting for Atlanta:

> It was fighting, fighting, every day. When we awoke in the morning, the firing of guns was our reveille, and when the sun went down it was our retreat and our lights out.

Women kept diaries that described life at home. Many were later published. Sarah Morgan was a loyal Southerner and a high-spirited young woman. When occupying Union forces forbade citizens to fly the Confederate flag in Baton Rouge, Louisiana, she wrote, "As soon as one is confiscated, I make another, until my ribbon is exhausted. . . . Hurrah! for the Bonny Blue Flag!"

Several generals, including Ulysses S. Grant and James Longstreet, wrote memoirs with detailed descriptions of their campaigns. Longstreet at Fredericksburg looked out at this sight:

> The flags of the Federals fluttered gayly, the polished arms shone brightly in the sunlight, and the beautiful uniforms of the buoyant troops gave to the scene the air of a holiday occasion. I could see almost every soldier [the enemy] had, and a splendid array it was. But off in the distance was Jackson's ragged infantry, and beyond was Stuart's battered cavalry, with their soiled hats and yellow butternut suits, a striking contrast to the handsomely equipped troops of the Federals.

After a battle, poet Walt Whitman searched army hospitals for his brother. When he saw the suffering of the wounded men, Whitman volunteered to serve as a nurse. He washed and fed and comforted the soldiers and wrote notes of

109

Alfred Waud sitting on a boulder sketching a battle scene

When war broke out, Ambrose Bierce was one of the first to enlist. At Shiloh, Chickamauga, and other battles, Bierce fought bravely and was promoted. At the war's end, he went to California and became a journalist and short-story writer. After revisiting the battlefields of his youth in 1913, Bierce left the country to witness the war then raging in Mexico. He was never heard from again, but he left behind his haunting stories of the Civil War.

Massachusetts novelist Louisa May Alcott served as a nurse during the war. She dedicated herself to the work until she contracted typhoid fever. She later wrote a book about her wartime nursing experience, *Hospital Sketches*.

Mark Twain, in his story "The Private History of a Campaign That Failed," tells how he enlisted, inspired by speeches "full of gunpowder and glory," and then spent most of his very short stint in the Confederate army hiding from the enemy in a farmer's corncrib.

One of the most faithful descriptions of the soldier's experience was written by a man who was born after the war, Stephen Crane. He wrote *The Red Badge of Courage*, the story of a soldier at Chancellorsville, after listening to old soldiers who had fought at that battle:

> The flames bit him, and the hot smoke broiled his skin. His rifle barrel grew so hot that ordinarily he could not have borne it upon his palms; but he kept stuffing cartridges into it, and pounding them with his clanking, bending ramrod.

his experiences. Whitman wrote many moving poems about the Civil War. In "Bivouac on a Mountain Side" he wrote:

> The numerous camp-fires scatter'd near and far, some away up on the mountain,
> The shadowy forms of men and horses, looming, large-sized, flickering,
> And over all the sky—the sky! far, far out of reach, studded, breaking out, the eternal stars.

ACTIVITY

Woodcut Prints

The sketches reporters drew from the battlefields were copied onto blocks of wood by engravers. The blocks were used to print line drawings for the newspapers, like Harper's Weekly, *which didn't print photographs in those times.*

What you need

Newspaper

½-inch thick piece of balsa wood, any size (found at craft or art supply stores)

Pencil

Bottle opener or other tools for carving (see suggestions below)*

Tempera paint

Paintbrush

Paper

Spread newspaper over your workspace. Lightly draw a design on the balsa wood with the pencil. For your first woodcut, draw a simple design—you'll want to practice before trying anything difficult. Using your bottle opener or any other tool you wish, scrape away the wood outside your design, pressing firmly so the tool cuts into the wood. Your design should stay raised while everything else is scraped away. The parts of the wood in "relief" (left raised) will be the parts that print. Paint the surface of the wood. Press it evenly and firmly onto your paper. Pull the wood piece straight up from the paper and set your printed page aside to dry. Paint the surface of the wood again to make more prints.

* Because balsa wood is so soft, almost anything can be used to carve designs into it. Get permission from an adult to use tools such as keys, orange peelers, fingernail files. You can hammer a bottle cap on the wood to make an indentation, use a paper clip to make fine lines, or use a screwdriver to make deeper ones.

Mathew Brady started his career as a graphic artist but became interested in a new medium—photography. Soon he was one of the most successful portrait photographers of his time, with several flourishing studios. When the war began, Brady had an idea. He wanted to photograph every aspect of the war, from the camps to the battlefields. He requested permission to accompany the Union army. Brady and his 20 assistants took over 3,000 photographs during the war. It was tricky work. Early photographers used several different processes to create images: "daguerreotypes" were printed on silver-plated metallic sheets; "ambrotypes" were made with glass coated with special chemicals; "tintypes" were made on thin sheets of iron. The equipment Brady's photographers used needed long exposure times. It was nearly impossible to get action shots of battles. They had to wait until the battles were over to take their photographs.

Many historians have written about the Civil War. There are full-length histories, dictionaries, atlases of battles, biographies of generals, and histories of regiments. People have devoted their lives to understanding the events of this era and sharing their findings with others.

The historians, novelists, artists, photographers, and just plain folks who recorded their experiences of the war have given us a great gift. Because of them, we can reach back over the years and gain an understanding of what it was like to have lived through this important era.

Tell a Story with Pictures

Mathew Brady and his assistants did more than just take pictures. Their work became a photographic history of the war. Fortunately, many of these photographs survived. They are among the war's most moving documents.

What you need

Camera

Film

Create your own photojournalism project. Use your imagination! Think of a topic or story you'd like to portray, and take a series of candid photos that illustrate the story. For example, get permission to shoot behind the scenes at a local wildlife or animal shelter, or take photographs of a school play, from tryouts to the final cast party. You can display your photos in book form, in a sequence that tells the story, or put on an exhibit in a visible area of your home or school, creating a "gallery" like those where Mathew Brady exhibited his photographs.

Two photographers having lunch

112

rom a mountaintop near the Rapidan River, Confederate General Robert E. Lee looked through his field glasses. Below, in his army's camp, 62,000 men waited. They were hungry and ragged but still devoted to their gray-haired general and the cause. To the east were the fords the Yankees had crossed a year ago. The Southerners had soundly defeated the Union army then, at Chancellorsville, Virginia. Lee guessed the Yankees would return. This time they would have a new leader.

The soldiers of the Union Army of the Potomac were eager to see their new commanding officer. So many commanders had come and gone. McClellan, Pope, Burnside, Hooker—they'd all been beaten by Robert E. Lee. Now Ulysses S. Grant was promoted to Lieutenant General, and in command of all the Union armies. He wanted to personally lead the Army of the Potomac, and not just run the war from an office in Washington. When he appeared at their camp, the soldiers looked the rumpled commander up and down. "Grant looks like a fighter," some said, but others replied, "Wait till he meets Bobby Lee and his boys."

Grant was impatient to meet Lee. He made his headquarters with George Meade and the Army of the Potomac and, in early May, led the 118,000-strong army over the Rapidan River and into the Wilderness. Grant hoped to get to open ground before challenging Lee, but Lee had other plans. He sent his troops against the Union forces in the dense and tangled Wilderness.

Battle of the Wilderness— May 5 through 6, 1864

When the forces first collided, Union commanders were sure they'd met the rear of a retreating Confederate army. When they met another corps, they changed their minds—this was a full-fledged attack. Grant sent his men forward. The soldiers grappled beneath the trees while the officers shouted commands. The fight was fearful and confusing. Bullets slammed into trees, and men lost their way in the dark forests. The battle lasted till nightfall, when the exhausted soldiers fell asleep on their arms. A Rebel corps under General Longstreet, still far from the battlefield, didn't get to sleep that night, but made a long march in the darkness to join their weary comrades.

A dawn attack by the Union sent the Confederates falling back. Robert E. Lee's headquarters was in danger as the Yankees moved closer, fighting their way through the undergrowth. Lee could see snatches of blue through the trees. Bullets whizzed past. Just as things looked most desperate, Longstreet's corps appeared.

The Texan Brigade, known for its ferocity in battle, was with them. General Lee once proudly described this brigade, saying, "Never mind the raggedness. The enemy never sees the backs of my Texans." Now he waved his hat in the air and shouted "Drive out these people!" He urged his horse Traveller forward to lead them in battle. The Texans wouldn't let their general risk his life. They shouted "Lee to the rear!" Yelling in fury, they entered the battle and threw their enemies aside. Half of the Texans were wounded or killed.

As Longstreet rode forward to direct an assault, shots rang out. Near the same ground where Stonewall Jackson had been struck by friendly fire a year before, James Longstreet was accidentally shot by his own men. He survived, but his wound kept him out of action for more than five months.

By the time the Confederates recovered from the shock, the Union troops had entrenched. The Rebels threw themselves at their enemy's fortifications. Sparks from shells started a fire in the woods, which spread to the Union breastworks. The soldiers fired at each other through a wall of flame. One last grand effort brought Confederate soldiers over the Union line, but darkness brought an end to the battle. Confederate casualties were 7,800; the Union army suffered more than 17,000. That night, Ulysses S. Grant wept in his tent.

In the morning, the Union forces prepared

An officer and his men on the field of battle

WOODCUT FROM *HARPER'S WEEKLY*

Battle of Spotsylvania—May 8 through 12, 1864

Their destination, Spotsylvania Courthouse, was a crossroads on the way to Richmond, Virginia. Robert E. Lee guessed his opponent's plans. He ordered his cavalry to Spotsylvania, and they held it until the infantry arrived. By the time the Union army arrived in Spotsylvania, the Confederate soldiers waited behind strong fortifications. At their center, these fortifications curved outward. The soldiers called this projecting line the "Mule Shoe" because of its shape.

General Grant sent 18,000 men in a dawn attack against the Mule Shoe. The Confederates barely saw their attackers approaching through the fog before they were on them. The Yankees forced their way into the Mule Shoe and took thousands of prisoners. Lee ordered reinforcements; Grant sent more men into the fray. For 18 hours, the men struggled for possession of the bend. Rain fell in torrents. Covered in mud and blood, the soldiers struggled desperately. When ammunition failed, they used bayonets. A bend where the fight was worst became a nightmare known as the Bloody Angle. The fight raged from dawn until midnight, when the Rebels fell back to a new defense line.

Much had been lost and little gained. Union casualties at Spotsylvania were a frightening 18,000 men. The Confederates suffered 10,000 casualties. When further assaults failed, Grant sent out orders for a march. He would try to find a better place to engage his enemy. He flanked Lee's army again and headed south.

to move. "Another skedaddle," many thought, predicting a retreat and another new commander. Grant surprised them all by pointing them south. He would go around Lee's army and try again; he wasn't finished fighting yet. When his men realized they were marching south and not in retreat, their spirits rose. They'd never had a general like this one, and even though they'd suffered in this battle, they felt they could win in another. The soldiers cheered Grant and sang as they marched.

While the infantrymen fought at Spotsylvania, their cavalry struggled at the gates of Richmond. Union cavalry (now led by hard-driving Philip Sheridan) clashed with Jeb Stuart's Rebel horsemen in a terrific battle at Yellow Tavern. Jeb Stuart was fatally wounded, and Lee grieved, saying, "I can scarcely think of him without weeping."

Grant tried to move around the Confederate army, but Lee moved faster. The Rebels dug in on the high bank of the North Anna River before the Army of the Potomac arrived. Several assaults against this position convinced General Grant that the Confederate line was too strong. Again, he flanked the Rebels. A move, a skirmish, and another flanking movement took them to Cold Harbor.

Cold Harbor—June 3, 1864

The armies faced each other along a seven-mile line. Though outnumbered, Robert E. Lee's men held good ground. As the Union soldiers advanced on the Confederates, none of them realized how perfectly fortified the Rebel lines were. The Confederate soldiers were silent until the enemy was near. Then, with a huge roar and a cloud of smoke, they opened fire. Whole companies dissolved in the "dreadful storm of lead and iron." The attack was brief but devastating. Seven thousand Union soldiers fell within minutes. Grant's officers couldn't bring themselves to send their soldiers in again. Both Lee and Grant were shocked at the outcome. Grant said, "I regret this assault more than any one I ever ordered."

Though devastated by the events at Cold Harbor, Ulysses S. Grant still refused to retreat. His depleted army moved south once again, withdrawing in the night.

This time, Grant surprised his opponent. Lee thought the Union soldiers were marching on the Confederate capital, Richmond. He turned his army toward that city. Grant, however, was moving against Petersburg, Virginia. This large city was a critical railroad junction. If Petersburg was captured, Richmond too would fall, for many of its supplies came through Petersburg. Grant's army moved quickly. The James River, nearly a half-mile wide at this point, wasn't even an obstacle. Union engineers constructed a 2,100-foot pontoon bridge in eight short hours and the army crossed the river.

The first Union troops to reach the outskirts of Petersburg were shocked to find it a fortress. There were 10 miles of earthworks, ditches, and fortifications, and a half-mile of empty ground that would have to be crossed under enemy fire. They tested the strength of the forbidding fortifications. A new unit of black troops, eager to prove their worth, raced across the ground, moved over the earthworks, and took prisoners and guns. Nightfall ended this promising start. The Yankees didn't know that if they'd kept advancing they could have taken the whole city. Petersburg was held by an anxious Pierre Beauregard, with only 2,200 men.

The White House Is Threatened

Robert E. Lee tried to divert Grant from Petersburg by sending General Jubal Early with a force against Washington. After besting Union troops in Maryland, Early's men came within five miles of the White House! General Grant sent a corps to the rescue. They arrived only just in time, and held Jubal Early off at one of Washington's forts. Lincoln visited the fort and, curious to see the Rebels, looked over a parapet. Bullets whizzed past his tall stovepipe hat.

A captain, who didn't recognize the president, shouted, "Get down, you fool, before you get shot!" Lincoln smiled and quickly obeyed. Jubal Early's forces retreated, but still threatened Washington from the Shenandoah Valley.

At last word reached General Lee that Grant's troops were at Petersburg, and he hurried to move his army there. Pierre Beauregard's men cheered when joined by their comrades. Union assaults against the fortifications the following day were fruitless. Grant had hoped to take the city by force, but now saw that it must be taken by siege.

Atlanta Falls— September 2, 1864

On the same day that Grant entered the Wilderness, Northern General William Tecumseh Sherman moved his army from their camp in Tennessee toward Joseph Johnston's Confederate army in Georgia. In the same way that Grant flanked Lee, but with much less loss of life, Sherman flanked Johnston. He side-stepped Johnston all the way to Atlanta, Georgia. Time after time, Sherman went around his enemy and threatened his rear, avoiding the head-on battle Johnston was trying to force. Each time Johnston stopped for a fight, Sherman went around him, from the town of Dalton to Resaca, from Resaca to Cassville, and from Cassville to Allatoona Pass.

With each movement, Sherman's army drew closer to Atlanta, Georgia. Atlanta was the second-largest city of the Confederacy, a huge railroad hub, and a manufacturing center that the South depended on for munitions and supplies. The Confederates burned bridges and destroyed railroad tracks, hoping to slow the Union advance, but the Yankees quickly repaired them and moved forward again. Sherman used the railroads and Northern supply depots to sustain his advancing army.

General Johnston always placed his troops in strong defensive positions, but Sherman wasn't interested in throwing his men against an entrenched enemy. When they reached Kennesaw Mountain, however, Sherman couldn't see a way around the Rebel army.

Figuring the Confederates weren't expecting a frontal attack, William Sherman sent his men straight in against the enemy's center. This was dangerous, but perhaps the element of surprise could take the day. The battle started with an "artillery barrage," an hour-long rain of shells. Then the Union soldiers advanced in a long line. As they grew closer to the entrenched Rebels, they came under crippling fire. The Yankees suffered terrible casualties as they tried to charge the entrenchments. The attack was a failure. A few days later, Sherman found a way to slip around the side of Johnston's army once again.

One hot July day the armies came to the very edge of Atlanta. Panicking citizens hurriedly packed their belongings onto wagons and left the city. The Confederate president Jefferson Davis was in a panic too. Johnston was doing his best to stop the Yankee advance, but Davis could only see that the Union army had invaded Georgia. How could Johnston have let the enemy advance so far? Atlanta was too important to sacrifice. Davis replaced Joseph Johnston with John Bell Hood.

John Bell Hood

John Bell Hood was a fighting man. Born in Kentucky, he attended West Point and fought on the nation's frontier. When his home state didn't secede, he enlisted from Texas and led the ferocious Texas Brigade. The tall, thin fighter lost the use of his arm at Gettysburg and had a leg amputated at Chickamauga, but nothing stopped him from serving his beloved Confederacy.

General Hood came out swinging. He smashed into Union troops just as they crossed Peachtree Creek near Atlanta. Though the fighting was furious, Hood was unable to budge the Yankees. Two days later, he sent a corps on a long night march to attack Union forces from the rear. It seemed as if the Rebels came in from all directions. In the confusion, a Union general rode into a Confederate force and, ordered to surrender, wheeled his horse to escape. He was killed. Confederate troops broke through Union lines here and there, but always the Union soldiers pushed them back, enraged by the loss of a commander. Hood's attacks came to nothing. He lost more than twice as many men as Sherman had, a percentage he couldn't afford. He withdrew to Atlanta.

Atlanta was fortified, and rather than throw his army against the city's earthworks, Sherman planned to take it by siege. Several of the rail-

Soldiers in trenches before battle

Ruins of Atlanta,
1864

roads that entered the city had already been destroyed. Only one line, to the south of Atlanta, remained to supply the troops and remaining citizens. Sherman sent a force around the city to destroy this railroad line. On the way, they clashed with a corps Hood sent to stop them. The Confederate soldiers charged valiantly, but were thrown back by the Yankees. Sherman spent a month lobbing shells into Atlanta, hoping the fire and short supplies would force a surrender. His soldiers destroyed the last railroad line into the city. They pulled up sections of track and heated the rail ties in bonfires. They twisted the heated ties into loops (which they laughingly called "Sherman hairpins") so they could never be used again. Nothing more would come into Atlanta from that direction.

General Hood tried one last time to drive the Yankees away, but the two corps he sent against them were thrown back and suffered great losses. Hood and his army evacuated the city. The next day, Union soldiers marched into it and William Tecumseh Sherman sent a telegram to Lincoln declaring that "Atlanta is ours."

The Union troops remained in Atlanta for two months. John Bell Hood went to Tennessee to destroy Sherman's supply lines and try to draw him back north, but Sherman decided he didn't need a supply line. His men would live off the land. Sherman would make his next attack not against an army but against the land that had supported it. He would lead his men on a march through Georgia all the way to the sea. Along the way they would cripple the country so it would

A black family entering Union lines

had told the mayor of Atlanta, "When peace does come, you may call on me for anything. Then will I share with you the last cracker." In the meantime, he said, "War is cruelty, and the crueler it is, the sooner it will be over." Across Georgia, the soldiers tore up railroad lines, made "Sherman hairpins," and burned barns, crops, and bridges.

As the army marched, slaves left the plantations to join them. Nearly 25,000 slaves accompanied Sherman's army as it cut through the South.

At Petersburg, Virginia, Robert E. Lee's worst fears had come true. "It will become a siege," he had predicted, "and then it will be a mere question of time." The Confederate army settled in behind their fortifications, outnumbered by the Yankees' forces facing them. The Northerners made repeated assaults against the Rebel lines. In the hot days of summer, the armies fought over control of railroads and roads leading into the city. In one attempt, Gettysburg hero Joshua Lawrence Chamberlain was badly wounded. He managed to stand long enough to wave his men forward in attack, then collapsed and was thought to be dead. His obituary appeared in the newspapers, but he survived his wounds to prove it wrong and fight another day. For his bravery, General Grant promoted him to brigadier general.

Over time, Grant extended his line around Petersburg, knowing that Lee would be forced to spread his line out too. With many fewer soldiers, Lee's army would be too thin to hold against a concentrated attack. As Grant reached around

no longer be able to supply its armies. He turned away from Hood, and, setting fire to Atlanta, set off through Georgia with the smoke of the city rising behind him.

From Atlanta to Savannah, Sherman's 60,000 men marched in wide columns. Parties of foragers (called "bummers") spread through the countryside, confiscating food for the vast army. What they didn't use, they destroyed. Sherman ordered his soldiers not to harm women, children, or unarmed men, but to destroy their land and property and their ability to wage war. He

121

The Crater

Pennsylvania soldiers, former coal miners, set to work to break through the Petersburg lines. They dug a 500-foot tunnel and filled it with four tons of gunpowder. They set off a blast beneath Rebel fortifications that created a crater 30 feet deep, 60 feet wide, and 170 feet long. Union soldiers were supposed to advance around the crater to attack, but instead they ran into it. Once in, they couldn't climb back up its steep slopes. Rebels fired on them from the front and sides. Thousands were taken prisoner, officers were condemned for the action, and Grant called the incident of the crater "the saddest affair I have witnessed in this war."

Petersburg, he cut off its roads. Eventually the Army of the Potomac was entrenched in a long arc, nearly surrounding the city.

Meanwhile, in Mobile Bay, the spirited Admiral Farragut moved his fleet of ships past blasting Confederate artillery. It was the last port in the Gulf of Mexico open to Confederate blockade-runners, and he was determined to take it. The bay was protected by gunboats, forts, and the ironclad C.S.S. *Tennessee*. Underwater mines, called "torpedoes," were planted at its entrance. Farragut's first ship hit a torpedo and, with a blast, sank to the depths! The others reversed their course to avoid the same fate. The fleet was pounded with shot and canister from the fort. Lashed to his mast, Farragut ordered his pilot to bring his ship past the others to lead them into the bay. An officer warned him of the dangerous mines, but Farragut shouted, "Damn the torpedoes! Full speed ahead!". The Confederate guns poured fire, and smoke filled the air. Farragut's ship struck hidden mines but they failed to go off. His fleet entered the bay and riddled the *Tennessee* with shot until the ironclad sent up the white flag of truce.

Farragut's victory was welcome news in the North, whose forces had suffered in the last months. Some Northern civilians were ready to give up on war and recognize the Confederacy as a separate country. An election was coming up and Lincoln's opponent in the "Peace Party" was the popular former leader of the Army of the Potomac, George McClellan. Lincoln hoped the country could be restored before it was too late.

In the meantime, the siege at Petersburg dragged on and Confederate General Jubal Early still threatened Washington. In the Shenandoah Valley, Early attacked Union troops. He even sent two cavalry brigades to Pennsylvania, where they set fire to Chambersburg. He had to be

Farragut in Mobile Bay

stopped. In August, Ulysses S. Grant put this job in the hands of Philip Sheridan. Destroy Early, he instructed Sheridan, and destroy the Shenandoah Valley at the same time. "Nothing should be left to invite the enemy to return," Grant said. If the rich agricultural land was destroyed, it could no longer feed and support the Confederate forces, who had used this route so often to successfully threaten Washington.

At the town of Winchester, Virginia, Union general Philip Sheridan's forces overcame the Confederates. Early moved up the Shenandoah Valley and they battled again. Sheridan surprised the Confederate forces with attacks from two sides. Again Jubal Early was forced to retreat. Sheridan turned his attention to the other half of Grant's instructions. He sent his troops up the Shenandoah Valley, and they burned crops, barns, and mills. Nothing would be left to support a Confederate army in this land.

Jubal Early had only half the troops Philip Sheridan commanded, but that didn't stop him from striking. The Rebels made a night march toward a Union encampment at Cedar Creek, Virginia. They charged the Yankees at dawn, taking hundreds of surprised prisoners while the rest of the Union soldiers fell back in confused retreat.

Fifteen miles away, General Sheridan woke to the sound of distant gunfire. He was on his way back to his army after a meeting in Washington. He hurriedly mounted his horse, Rienzi, and galloped toward the gunfire. Along the way, he met groups of his men in retreat. The feisty general shouted at them to follow him back to the battlefield. The soldiers were inspired by their bold leader, and they gathered together for a counterstrike. When the armies met for the second time that day, the Rebel soldiers were finally defeated. Sheridan had removed any further threats from the Shenandoah Valley. Eventually, he took his troops to help General Grant at Petersburg.

With the good news from Atlanta, Mobile Bay, and the Shenandoah Valley, the Northern people had new hope for victory and reunion. Abraham Lincoln won the election in a landslide. At his inauguration he set the stage for future reunion with the Confederacy. "With malice toward none; with charity for all; with firmness in the right, as God gives us to see the right, let us strive on to finish the work we are in; to bind up the nation's wounds; to care for him who shall have borne the battle, and for his widow, and his orphan—to do all which may achieve and cherish a just, and a lasting peace, among ourselves, and with all nations."

14

Taps

The siege of Petersburg, Virginia, lasted 10 long months, from June 1864 to April 1865. The soldiers spent more time digging than shooting, and eventually a line of trenches reached 37 miles around Richmond and Petersburg. Outside Petersburg, Union soldiers built redoubts and redans, zigzag trenches, saps, and bomb-proof shelters complete with chimneys. On both sides, iron balls screamed overhead at all hours of the day.

At first the constant shelling was nerve-wracking. After a time, ducking shells seemed not at all unusual. As one Yankee described it, when the soldiers heard shells coming overhead, "business of a very pressing nature suddenly called us into the bombproofs."

The Union supply base was as big as a city. Hospitals were built for the wounded, and warehouses were constructed to hold the many supplies needed for the large Union army. Engineers built a railroad from the nearby James River to bring in the supplies. Fall came, then winter, and it seemed as if the siege would never end.

In the meantime, Sherman continued his march from Atlanta to the sea. Confederate General John Bell Hood knew he couldn't stop Sherman's large army, so he turned his own Army of Tennessee toward Nashville. Union

A Gift for an Enemy

When General Grant heard that Confederate opponent Pierre Beauregard had a newborn son, he had his men fire off a salute and sent a gift of silverware across the battle lines.

general George Thomas had been assigned to hold that city. Hood hoped to defeat Thomas, then move east to go to Robert E. Lee's assistance. Many of the men in Hood's army were from Tennessee, and were pleased to be marching back to their home state.

Battle of Franklin— November 30, 1864

On the road to Nashville, they ran into a 28,000-man Union force. General Hood tried to attack the Yankees from two sides, but they slipped away from him. Hood, furious, pushed his men after the enemy toward the town of Franklin. When the Confederates reached Franklin, they found that the Union soldiers had dug in and were safely behind their fortifications. In spite of the Union's greater strength and their entrenched position, General Hood ordered his officers to "drive the enemy from his position." The assault he ordered would bring his own army to its knees.

His 18,000 men crossed a wide field in front of their enemies, through air "loaded with death-dealing missiles." In charge after charge, the Confederates threw themselves against the entrenched Yankees. In a fight as fierce as any that had been fought in the war, they struggled for hours. Six Confederate generals were killed, more than in any other battle. The Army of Tennessee suffered 7,000 casualties. One young Tennessee soldier, who hadn't been home in so long, died in

the yard of his family's home, which stood in the middle of the battlefield. The battle raged until midnight, when the Union troops pulled back, crossed the river, and marched to Nashville.

Though his army was crippled, John Bell Hood followed the Union force to Nashville. There was nothing he could do there against the much larger Union army, so he lined up his men south of the city and waited. Two weeks later, General George Thomas brought his Union army out of Nashville to fight. In a dawn attack, they created a diversion on the Rebel right and center while striking with great force against the left. The Confederates struggled to hold their ground. When the Union renewed its attack the next day, the Confederate Army of Tennessee completely collapsed. Some of its men surrendered; others fled south.

In the meantime, Sherman's army had marched to the sea. In late December, they conquered and entered Savannah, Georgia. Sherman sent another telegram to Lincoln. "I beg to present you as a Christmas gift," he said, "the city of Savannah with 150 heavy guns, plenty of ammunition and 25,000 bales of cotton." When they left that city, they cut an even wider path through South Carolina. This had been the first state to secede, and the soldiers hadn't forgotten that fact. They destroyed the city of Columbia. Only chimneys were left standing in the wake of their advance. Joseph Johnston, recently appointed to command the forces in the Carolinas, tried in vain to stop William Sherman's advance.

In Petersburg, Virginia, Robert E. Lee's Confederate army had been depleted during the long siege. Those remaining were starving. They couldn't survive much longer. Lee had to try something to save his army and the Confederacy, even if it meant abandoning Petersburg and Richmond. He made a plan to escape from the besieged city, join forces with Joseph Johnston, and beat first Sherman, then Grant. It was the Confederacy's only hope.

The Fall of Richmond, Virginia, on the Night of April 2nd 1865

The fighting around Petersburg, Virginia had grown fiercer. Just as General Lee was planning his next move, thousands of his men were taken prisoner at the crossroads of Five Forks, southwest of Petersburg. Grant, to follow up on this success, ordered an assault all along the Petersburg lines. Hours before dawn, the Union attack began, and the Confederates were driven out of their trenches around the city. Confederate General Ambrose Powell Hill, as he rode to rally his troops, fell into the hands of Union soldiers. As he lifted his sword and called on them to surrender, he was shot and fell dead from his horse.

When the Confederate soldiers poured in from their defenseworks, Lee knew the time had come to give up the city. From the house that served as his headquarters in Petersburg, he sent a telegram to Jefferson Davis. His troops were leaving Petersburg, Lee told his president, and "Richmond must be evacuated this evening." Lee buckled his sword around his waist and mounted his horse Traveller. He rode away under cannon fire.

The Confederate government moved quickly to abandon its capital. Jefferson Davis boarded a train and left Richmond to head south for safety. Davis's family had left the city days before but Lee's wife, Mary, stayed behind. The Confederate troops who had been posted at Richmond were instructed to join Lee at Amelia Courthouse, 40 miles west of Petersburg. As they left Richmond, they set fire to warehouses, bridges, and ships to keep them out of the hands

Lincoln Visits Richmond

Abraham Lincoln was visiting General Grant's headquarters when Petersburg fell. With his wife and Tad, he had come to see how his army was faring, and to check on his son Robert, who was on Grant's staff. When the city was evacuated, he followed Grant in for a look at it. Two days after Richmond's fall, he was eager for a look at that city too. He took a boat upriver, accompanied by a small guard of marines and his son Tad, who was greatly enjoying this adventure on his twelfth birthday. They walked through streets past crowds of Southerners shocked by the sight of the tall president. Former slaves flocked to Lincoln with thanks and praise.

At the White House of the Confederacy, Lincoln sat at Davis's desk. Later that day, Lincoln asked a band to play "Dixie." "That tune is now Federal property," he joked.

of the Union army, who would soon be entering the capital. Wind caught the fires and they spread throughout the city, burning homes and buildings. An arsenal caught on fire with an explosion that rocked the ground.

While Grant prepared a force to follow Lee, he ordered other troops to occupy Richmond. A regiment of black cavalry was the first Union force to enter the Confederate capital. They put out the raging fires and posted a guard at Mrs. Lee's door for her safety. The Confederate White House became a Union headquarters.

General Lee's Army of Northern Virginia marched west to Amelia Courthouse. Lee had ordered a supply of rations to be sent to the train station there to feed his hungry men. From that point, he hoped to lead them south to join Joseph Johnston's forces in North Carolina. He had to move quickly. Union cavalry forces were hot on his heels, and the infantry was not far behind them.

When the Confederates reached their destination, the 55,000 hungry and tired soldiers were dismayed to find that their rations hadn't arrived. Lee sent foragers to comb the countryside. He lost one day's lead while they searched for food. They found little. While they foraged, the Union troops advanced and blocked the roads leading south so that Lee was unable to join Joseph Johnston. Forced in another direction,

Lee ordered his men west. The starving soldiers stumbled along dark roads on grueling night marches. Lee arranged for rations to be sent to another town ahead, Appomattox Courthouse, if only his poor soldiers could make it that far.

The Union troops moved quickly to block Lee again. While the Rebel soldiers stumbled along, the Yankees marched double-quick. Lee's rear was struck by Union forces, who captured 6,000 soldiers of the dwindling Confederate army, including General Richard Ewell and Lee's son, Custis. The next day the Rebels barely held off a Union infantry attack, then made another long night march.

The Confederate soldiers were exhausted by the night marches, and each had only a handful of parched corn to last through the days. Many had fallen by the roadsides. Others dropped their weapons and blankets and stumbled along blindly. Though they made terrific efforts to get to Appomattox Courthouse first, when they arrived there they found that Union cavalry had beaten them. The cavalry stood between them and the supply trains they'd marched so long to meet. The Confederates didn't know how many troopers faced them, but after meeting with his officers, Lee ordered an assault for the next day. There was nowhere left for them to go. They could only fight or surrender.

McLean House

Wilmer McLean had a home near Manassas that was shelled badly during the first battle of the war. He moved, saying he wanted to live where his family would never again be bothered by war. By a strange coincidence, the war ended in his new home at Appomattox Courthouse.

In the morning, the hungry, exhausted, but still devoted Confederate soldiers moved against the Union cavalry. Letting loose with a Rebel yell, they ran over the enemy lines. The Yankees fell back in retreat, and for a moment the hearts of the Confederate soldiers were glad. Then they looked up and their hearts sank. Columns of Union infantry approached in great numbers.

Just as the Union infantry began their advance, a Confederate officer galloped across the lines. He carried a white flag of truce and a message for General Grant, asking him to meet General Lee to discuss terms of surrender.

The generals met in the parlor of Wilmer McLean's home. General Lee looked splendid in his best uniform. General Grant apologized

McLean House

Memorial Day

Memorial Day (or Decoration Day) was created in 1868 to honor those who died fighting the war. Now on this holiday we honor all soldiers who fought in American wars. Another way people honor Civil War veterans is by reenacting battles.

Hundreds of reenactments are held throughout the United States every year. Attend one and see for yourself what a Civil War battle was like. Participants live in encampments exactly like those of the Civil War, and they act out real battles. They try hard to be sure that everything is authentic, from their rifle-muskets to their uniforms. Tour the camps and talk to the soldiers as they clean weapons and cook dinner. Visit the sutlers, and see doctors in medical tents as they tend to the wounded.

for his muddy boots and rumpled private's jacket. They talked briefly of having met during the Mexican War, then Lee reminded Grant of their reason for meeting this day. General Grant offered generous terms of surrender. The Confederates would surrender their arms, and give an oath that they would never again take them up against the United States government. They would not be punished for having gone to war. The men would be allowed to keep their horses, Grant added, to help them plant their crops when they went home to their farms. "This will have the best possible effect," said Lee, "It will do much toward conciliating our people."

When Grant heard that the Confederate army had no provisions, he ordered 25,000 rations to be sent to their lines. The generals shook hands and Lee rode back to his men. Grant left for his headquarters and, as he rode, Union guns were set off in celebration of the victory. General Grant ordered them stopped out of respect for their former enemies. "The war is over," he said, "The Rebels are our countrymen again."

Robert E. Lee's men cheered him as he returned to their lines. When they saw his face, they knew it was over. Tears filled his eyes. As Traveller moved through the crowds of soldiers, the men reached out to touch their beloved general's horse. In his farewell orders to his army, General Lee praised them for their unsurpassed courage and thanked them for their devotion.

At a ceremony three days later, the Southerners marched to a field at Appomattox to surrender their colors and their weapons. Union general Joshua Lawrence Chamberlain watched as Stonewall Jackson's old brigade approached to stack their arms. Chamberlain was moved by the sight of these brave men who had sacrificed so much over the years of war. He ordered his men to "carry arms," a salute of honor, as the brigade marched past. The Confederate soldiers returned the salute.

The surrender of the Army of Northern Virginia spelled the end of the Confederacy. In North Carolina, Joseph Johnston surrendered his forces to General Sherman. In Alabama, Nathan Bedford Forrest surrendered. (The cavalry leader, who had killed 30 men during the war and had had 29 horses shot out from under him, said he was "a horse ahead.") In Georgia, Jefferson Davis was captured by Union cavalry as he tried to make his way to the west. The last battle of the war was fought in Texas. It was a Confederate victory, but it was clear to the Rebel commanders in Texas that they couldn't hold out any longer. The western armies, too, laid down their arms. The very last Confederate general to surrender was Brigadier General Stand Watie, a Cherokee Indian who had sided with the South and served it boldly. Some were bitter, some were sad, some just relieved to be done with war.

Church bells rang all over the North, and in Washington there were fireworks and hundred-gun salutes. No one was happier to see the end of war than President Lincoln. Crowds gathered at the White House and begged for a speech. His

Box in Ford's Theater where Lincoln was assassinated

words were of healing and of a united future. Then once again, he asked a band to play "Dixie."

On April 14, 1865, Robert Anderson, who had surrendered Fort Sumter to the Confederacy so long ago, raised the Stars and Stripes over the fort once more. The watching crowd cheered for the Union and for Lincoln. In Washington, their president was on his way to Ford's Theater, to enjoy a light-hearted evening with his wife now that the nation's troubles were over.

Lincoln was killed by an assassin's bullet at Ford's Theater that night. John Wilkes Booth, a famous actor, was embittered by the Confederacy's loss, and took revenge on the nation by taking the life of its great president. He shot Lincoln in his box at the theater and jumped to the stage, shouting "The South is avenged!" Booth escaped by the stage door and jumped on a waiting horse. Lincoln was carried to a house across the street and died there early the next morning. People across the nation mourned for their great president.

Booth was captured as he hid in a Virginia tobacco barn, and killed when he refused to surrender. Others who had conspired with him to kill the president were found guilty and hanged.

The country would face hard years as the people of the North and South learned to be one nation again. For now, the men who had fought so long and so hard were looking homeward. The Southern soldiers walked back to their farms and families. Many had nothing left to sustain them on the journey. People in towns across the South shared their meager meals with the brave men who had fought for them. Union soldiers, before they went home, gathered in Washington for a Grand Review. For two days, 200,000 soldiers paraded before thousands of spectators, their general-in-chief, Ulysses S. Grant, and the new president, Andrew Johnson. With loud cheers, the crowd thanked them for their sacrifices.

The soldiers of the North and South went home changed men. Their memories of battle and of fallen comrades would never leave them.

The United States was a new country. The 13th Amendment to the Constitution was passed, stating that "neither slavery nor involuntary servitude shall exist" in this nation that was united once more. The years of battle and bloodshed had recreated the United States. In its bloody rebirth, the country became a nation that stood for its principles of democracy and freedom. The war was over. The soldiers and their officers, the women and children at home, all those once divided, North and South, were all countrymen again.

The Last Veterans

Over 10,000 military engagements were fought in the Civil War. Approximately three million Americans served. More than 620,000 died during the war. Pleasant Crump, considered to be the last surviving Confederate veteran, died in 1951. The last Union veteran of the war, a former drummer boy named Albert Woolson, died in 1956.

Scouting for Civil War Veterans

If your family has lived in the United States for a while, it's possible that one of your ancestors served in the Civil War. The best place to start a family history search is with your parents and grandparents. Ask them to tell you everything about your family, as far back in time as they know. Interview other family members who might have collected information about your family tree. If you have an old family Bible, check to see if anyone has written the names and birthdates of ancestors there.

Your parents' birth certificates will state your grandparents' names, birthdates, and birthplaces. Using this information, you can send away for the birth certificates of your grandparents from the states where they were born, and find out about their parents. With luck, you can go far back in time. Perhaps you'll find that you have an ancestor who lived during the time of the Civil War. If that person was a young man in the 1860s, there's a chance he was a soldier.

The Civil War Archives of the state your ancestor lived in may be able to tell you something about his unit and his military record. Ask a librarian to help you find the address of that state's archives. Send them a letter with a self-addressed, stamped envelope to ask how to get military or pension records. If your ancestor filled out a pension application, you may get a copy of that, which will tell the battles he fought in and if he was wounded or imprisoned. If you find out the regiment your ancestor served in, you may be able to gather information about that regiment's history in some of the many books about the Civil War.

The National Archives, for a $10 fee, will search for military or pension records if you know your ancestor's full name and his military unit. To get copies of the forms for this search, write to the National Archives, NNRG-C, Washington, D.C., 20408.

What Happened to Them After the War?

Frederick Douglass became U.S. minister to Haiti.

Clara Barton founded the American Red Cross.

Drummer boy Johnny Clem retired from the army in 1915 as a brigadier general.

Robert Smalls, the one-time slave who stole a ship for the Union, bought his former master's home and served five terms in the U.S. Congress.

Jefferson Davis was imprisoned for two years after his capture, then released with no trial.

William Tecumseh Sherman eventually became the U.S. Army's general-in-chief.

David Farragut became the U.S. Navy's first admiral.

George Armstrong Custer met his end at the Battle of Little Big Horn.

George McClellan lost his bid for the presidency but became governor of New Jersey.

Robert E. Lee became president of Washington College in Virginia (now known as Washington and Lee University).

Ulysses S. Grant became the 18th president of the United States.

Grand Review of Union troops

Glossary

The words here are defined as they are used in this book; they may have a more general meaning elsewhere.

Abatis: A fortification made of trees cut down so their branches face the enemy

Abolitionists: People who supported the abolishment of slavery in the United States

Artillery: Large guns such as mortars and cannons; the word "artillery" is also the name of the units armed with these guns

Battery: An artillery unit of from 70 to 100 men and 4 to 6 big guns

Bayonet: A knife fixed to the front end of a musket or rifle

Blockade: The use of military force to close ports

Breastworks: Chest-high fortifications made of dirt and wood

Bummers: Sherman's foraging soldiers, who commandeered items from southern communities

Campaign: A series of military operations that aim for a specific goal

Canister: A tin can that is filled with iron balls and shot from a cannon

Casualty: A person killed, wounded, captured, or missing in action after a battle

Cavalry: Sword-carrying troops who rode horses into battle

Colors: The flag of a country or of a military unit

Color-bearer: The soldier assigned to carry a unit's flag

Commandeer: To take possession because of military necessity

Commissary: The officer or department in charge of providing food for the army

Confederates: Southerners fighting for the Confederate States of America

Court-martial: A military court or a military trial

Demonstration/Diversion: To draw the attention of the enemy away from the main field of battle with an attack or skirmish

Deploy: To spread troops out to form a battle line

Draft: Required service in the military

Earthworks: Fortifications made of dirt

Emancipate: To set free from slavery

Enlist: To join the military

Entrenched: Gaining some protection from the enemy by fighting from ditches, or "trenches"

Federals: A name for soldiers fighting for the Union

Flank: The left or right side of an army's line; a "flank attack" is a side attack; "to flank" an enemy is to get around or in back of that enemy

Flotilla: A fleet of small vessels

Foraging: Searching for and seizing food and supplies

Gangrene: A local death of soft tissue in the body due to loss of blood supply to that area

Grape/grapeshot: Cast-iron pellets packed together for cannon shot

Gun: Big guns or cannons

Hardtack: A hard biscuit made of flour, salt, and water

Haversack: A canvas shoulder bag used to hold rations

Housewife: Cloth bag containing a sewing kit

Howitzer: A mid-range cannon with a medium-length barrel

Infantry: Soldiers who fought on foot, equipped with small arms

Ironclad: A warship covered with iron plating

Line of communications: See "supply line"

Mexican War: Mexico and the United States fought over control of Texas between 1846 and 1848. The war ended with Mexico yielding both Texas and California to the United States.

Militia/militiamen: Citizen soldiers called out for emergencies

Minié ball: A cone-shaped lead bullet designed for use in the rifle-barreled musket

Mortar: Short, stubby cannons used for lobbing shells into fortifications

Munitions: Ammunition

Napoleon: An artillery gun in common use during the Civil War

Orderly: A soldier who carried orders for officers

Ordnance: Weapons and related supplies; ordnance is also the name of the branch of the army responsible for weapons and related supplies

Parapet: A wall for the protection of troops

Picket: A soldier stationed to guard a camp or an army

Ration: A soldier's daily allowance of food

Rebel: A nickname for soldiers fighting for the Confederacy

Reveille: A morning bugle or drum call that let soldiers know it was time to wake up

Secession/Secede: Formal withdrawal from a union/to withdraw

Sharpshooter: An especially skilled rifleman

Shell: An iron cannon ball filled with an explosive charge

Shot: Solid iron balls shot from a cannon

Siege: To surround a city or enemy army, cutting off supplies, in order to force surrender

Skirmish: A light military action

States' rights: The idea that any power not granted to the federal government by the Constitution belongs to individual states, or that states may cancel an act of the government

Supply line: The route along which supplies and reinforcements come to the army, usually a road or a railroad

Sutler: A peddler who followed the armies to sell food and supplies to the soldiers

Terms of surrender: Conditions agreed to by commanding generals at surrender, such as imprisonment and surrender of arms

Theater: In war, a region that is the scene of military actions

Torpedo: During the Civil War, an underwater mine

West Point: The U.S. Military Academy in New York, founded in 1802

Yankees: A nickname for soldiers fighting for the Union

A Guide to Officers

Confederate Officers

Armistead, Lewis

Beauregard, Pierre Gustave Toutant

Bragg, Braxton

Early, Jubal

Ewell, Richard S.

Forrest, Nathan Bedford

Hill, Ambrose Powell

Hill, D. H.

Hood, John Bell

Jackson, Thomas J. ("Stonewall")

Johnston, Albert Sidney

Johnston, Joseph Eggleston

Lee, Robert E.

Longstreet, James

Magruder, John

Morgan, John Hunt

Mosby, John Singleton

Pickett, George

Polk, Leonidas

Stuart, James E. B. ("Jeb")

Van Dorn, Earl

Watie, Stand

Union Officers

Anderson, Robert

Burnside, Ambrose

Chamberlain, Joshua Lawrence

Custer, George Armstrong

Farragut, David Glascow

Grant, Ulysses S.

Hancock, Winfield Scott

Hooker, Joseph

McClellan, George

McDowell, Irvin

Meade, George Gordon

Pope, John

Rosecrans, William

Sedgwick, John

Sheridan, Philip

Sherman, William Tecumseh

Sickles, Dan

Sumner, Edwin

Thomas, George

Warren, Gouverneur K.

Resources

Battlefields, Important Sites, and Museums

Andersonville National Historic Site
Route 1, Box 800
Andersonville, Georgia, 31711
(912) 924-0343

In 1864, 32,000 Federal prisoners were held here.

Antietam National Battlefield
P.O. Box 158
Sharpsburg, Maryland 21782-0158
(301) 432-5124

The site of the bloodiest day of the Civil War.

Appomattox Court House National Historical Park
P.O. Box 218
Appomattox, Virginia 24522
(804) 352-8987

Site of the McLean house and the Surrender Triangle, where the Confederates stacked their arms.

Arlington House and National Cemetery
George Washington Memorial Parkway
McLean, Virginia 22101
(703) 557-0613

The burial place of 200,000 veterans and the one-time home of General Robert E. Lee.

The Black Heritage Trail of the Boston African-American National Historic Site
Abiel Smith School
46 Joy Street
Boston, Massachusetts 02114-4025
(617) 742-5415

The trail features a memorial to the 54th Massachusetts Regiment and an Underground Railroad station.

Chickamauga and Chattanooga National Military Park
3370 Lafayette Road
Fort Oglethorpe, Georgia 30742
(706) 866-9241

See the River of Blood and Lookout Mountain.

Ford's Theater National Historic Site
511 10th Street, NW
Washington, D.C. 20003
(202) 426-6924

The site of Lincoln's assassination also houses a Lincoln museum.

Fort Sumter National Monument
1214 Middle Street
Sullivan's Island, South Carolina 29482
(803) 883-3123

See where the first shots of the Civil War rang out.

Franklin Battlefield's Carter House
1140 Columbia Avenue
Franklin, Tennessee 37064
(615) 791-1861

Seven hundred bullet holes still mark the Carter House walls.

Fredericksburg and Spotsylvania National Military Parks
706 Caroline Street
Fredericksburg, Virginia 22401
(540) 371-0802

The site of the battles of Fredericksburg, Chancellorsville, the Wilderness, and Spotsylvania

Gettysburg National Military Park
97 Taneytown Road
Gettysburg, Pennsylvania 17325
(717) 334-1124

The biggest battle of the Civil War was fought here.

Harpers Ferry National Historic Park
P.O. Box 65
Harpers Ferry, West Virginia 25425
(304) 535-6298

Site of battles and John Brown's revolt

The Levi Coffin House
113 U.S. Highway 20
Fountain City, Indiana 47341
(765) 847-2432

A one-time station on the Underground Railroad

Manassas National Battlefield Park
12521 Lee Highway
Manassas, Virginia 20109
(703) 361-1339

The site of two important Civil War battles

The Mariners' Museum
100 Museum Drive
Newport News, Virginia 23606
(800) 581-7245

See objects salvaged from the U.S.S. *Monitor*—and more.

The Museum of the Confederacy
1201 East Clay Street
Richmond, Virginia 23219
(804) 649-1861

Holdings include Robert E. Lee's Appomattox sword and Jeb Stuart's plumed hat.

National Museum of Civil War Medicine
P.O. Box 470
Frederick, Maryland 21705
(301) 695-1864

A resource for everything you ever wanted to know about Civil War medicine, plus exhibits on recruitment and the home front

National Museum of the Civil War Soldier
Pamplin Historical Park
6125 Boydton Plank Road
Petersburg, Virginia 23803
(804) 861-2408

Multi-sensory exhibits show what it was really like to be in the Civil War.

Petersburg National Battlefield
1539 Hickory Hill Road
Petersburg, Virginia 23803-4721
(804) 732-3531

Includes reconstructed fortifications and trenches and the site of the Crater

Richmond National Battlefield Park
3215 East Broad Street
Richmond, Virginia 23223
(804) 226-1981

The site of the battles of the Seven Days and Cold Harbor

Shiloh National Military Park
Route 1, Box 9
Shiloh, Tennessee 38376
(901) 689-5696

Once the site of a bitter battle, now a "place of peace"

Vicksburg National Military Park
3201 Clay Street
Vicksburg, Mississippi 39180
(601) 636-0583

This park features battery stations and fortifications.

Web Sites to Explore

There are thousands of Web sites on the Civil War. Here are just a few of the best resource pages for a wide range of information on topics related to the Civil War.

Abraham Lincoln Online
www.netins.net/showcase/creative/lincoln.html

This site provides many links to resources on the president.

The American Civil War Home Page
sunsite.utk.edu/civil-war/warweb.html

This site offers information from regimental histories to letters by soldiers and lists of battle reenactments you can visit.

The American Civil War Home Page from Dakota State University
www.homepage.dsu.edu/jankej/civilwar/civilwar.htm

Learn about a variety of topics such as weapons, blacks in the war, prisons, and general battle histories.

Association for the Preservation of Civil War Sites
www.apcws.com

Visit this site to find out about junior membership and tours for kids sponsored by this organization devoted to saving historic Civil War battlefields!

Civil War Artillery
www.cwartillery.org/artillery.html

Everything you ever wanted to know about Civil War artillery.

General Lee's Headquarters
www.geocities.com/TimesSquare/Bunker/1048/second.html

Enter the tent of Confederate General Robert E. Lee at this site.

Harriet Tubman and the Underground Railroad
www2.lhric.org/pocantico/tubman/tubman.html

This is an informative site written by kids.

The Library of Congress
rs6.loc.gov/ammem/cwphome.html

Over 1,100 of Mathew Brady's photographs of the war can be seen at this Library of Congress site.

Link on Lincoln
www.cmi.k12.il.us/Urbana/projects/LinkOn/

For fun facts about Lincoln's life before he was president. This site was created by kids in Illinois.

Music of the Civil War
www.geocities.com/SouthBeach/Boardwalk/2575/civil.html

Listen to dozens of songs from the Civil War era.

The National Archives
www.nara.gov/exhall/exhibits.html

From here you can view original American documents including the Emancipation Proclamation and the police blotter that listed Lincoln's assassination.

National Park Service
www.cr.nps.gov/csd/gettex/

This site will take you on an interactive tour of a Civil War army camp.

Remember the Ladies
www.geocities.com/Heartland/4678/kate.html

This site features women's involvement in the Civil War.

The Ulysses S. Grant Home Page
www.mscomm.com/~ulysses/

This site offers tons of information about General Grant and allows students to ask questions.

The United States Civil War Center
www.cwc.lsu.edu/

This is a comprehensive database of all topics related to the Civil War.

United States Colored Troops in the Civil War
www.coax.net/people/lwf/data.htm

Histories of black regiments and individual black soldiers, as well the battles they fought in, can be found at this site.

The White House
www.whitehouse.gov/

This site provides presidential history and information on government, and has a special site for kids.

Bibliography

Bierce, Ambrose. *Civil War Stories*. New York: Dover Publications, 1994.

*Billings, John D. *Hard Tack and Coffee*. Lincoln, Nebraska: University of Nebraska Press, 1993.

Catton, Bruce. *The Civil War*. Boston: Houghton Mifflin Company, 1987.

Constable, George, ed. *Spies, Scouts, and Raiders*. Alexandria, Virginia: Time-Life Books, 1985.

Crane, Stephen. *The Red Badge of Courage*. New York: W.W. Norton & Company, 1976.

Donald, David Herbert. *Lincoln*. New York: Simon & Schuster, 1995.

Douglass, Frederick. *Autobiographies*. New York: The Library of America, 1994.

Foote, Shelby. *The Civil War, A Narrative*. New York: Vintage Books, 1986.

Freemantle, Arthur. *Three Months in the Southern States*. Lincoln, Nebraska: University of Nebraska Press, 1991.

Furgurson, Ernest B. *Chancellorsville 1863*. New York: Vintage Books, 1993.

*Hunt, Irene. *Across Five Aprils*. Chicago: Follett Publishing Company, 1964.

Jackson, Kennell. *America Is Me*. New York: HarperPerennial, 1997.

Johnson, Robert Underwood and Clarence Clough Buel, eds. *Battles and Leaders of the Civil War*. Secaucus, New Jersey: Castle Books, 1983.

Katcher, Philip. *The Civil War Source Book*. New York: Facts on File, 1992.

Kope, Spencer. *Everything Civil War*. Silverdale, Washington: Willow Creek Press, 1997.

MacDonald, John. *Great Battles of the Civil War*. New York: Collier Books, 1988.

McPherson, James M. *Battle Cry of Freedom*. New York: Ballantine Books, 1988.

Morgan, Sarah. *The Civil War Diary of a Southern Woman*. New York: Simon & Schuster, 1991.

Twain, Mark. *Tales, Speeches, Essays & Sketches*. New York: Penguin Books, 1994.

Ward, Geoffrey C., Ken Burns, and Ric Burns. *The Civil War*. New York: Alfred A. Knopf, 1991.

*Watkins, Sam R. *Co. Aytch: A Confederate Memoir of the Civil War*. New York: Touchstone Press, 1990.

Whitman, Walt. *Civil War Poetry and Prose*. New York: Dover Publications, 1995.

Wiley, Bell I. *The Life of Johnny Reb and The Life of Billy Yank*. New York: Book-of-the-Month Club, 1994.

*These books are especially recommended for young readers. *Across Five Aprils* is a fictional account of a boy's life during the Civil War. *Hard Tack and Coffee* and *Co. Aytch: A Confederate Memoir of the Civil War* are first-hand accounts by soldiers about life in the army.

Index

Page numbers in italics denote illustrations.